Social Skills
for kids 3 to 10

90 Fun Activities to Help Your Child Overcome Anxiety, Boost Self-Esteem, Make Friends, and Overcome Shyness

Written by Kate Herm

CONTENTS

INTRODUCTION

FOR THE GROWN-UP...

As a parent, you understand that every child in this world is different. Children have their own unique set of abilities, skills, and personalities. For example, some children excel in arithmetic, while others may need assistance. Some kids can take up a pencil and draw anything they want, while others need some guidance.

Kids have diverse capacities in social skills, just as they do with language, arithmetic, or art. Some kids may immediately detect other people's feelings, while others may need practice. Some children naturally make friends, while others must learn how to make friends. You are undoubtedly aware of where your kid stands in this area and where they may need some assistance. However, I am here to inform you that your child can learn this stuff, and it can drastically improve a child's confidence and social success.

Furthermore, like teaching arithmetic ideas or reading comprehension, you can break down social skills into manageable chunks that your kid can absorb and learn. Your kid may discover the vital social skills required to be socially successful at school, in family circumstances, and out and about in the community with the help of this book and you as a supporting guide.

Young children have access to various social circumstances at school and home, but they may not always have the experience or expertise to manage them.

Teaching your kid social life skills at a young age—between the ages of three and ten—provides many crucial advantages. Many studies suggest that excellent social skills help children minimize stress, play, collaborate with classmates, achieve higher academic performance, and form stronger connections with people around them.

You may educate your kid on social skills by playing engaging games at home, just like you teach them to count, recite the alphabet, and discover colors.

This book has more than 90 exercises intended to teach children the social skills they will need throughout their lives, such as:

- Communication
- Cooperation
- Responsibility
- Active listening
- Empathy
- Self-Control
- Engagement
- Problem-solving
- Emotional regulation
- Respect

Each project contains a list of supplies, the majority of which you are likely to already have on hand. You will also discover a concise overview of the activity, the number of participants required, where the action may be completed (indoor, outdoor, or online), and a list of the kids' abilities to master while engaging in the activity.

The step-by-step directions for setting up and completing the activity or game will help you get to the exciting parts faster! To get the most out of the activities, go through the reflection questions, which will urge kids to think about their experience playing the games and how they may use those abilities in other circumstances in their life.

These activities may be completed in a short time at home with family, with a bunch of friends in a playgroup, in the neighborhood, or even remotely with family and friends through video chat. The activities educate children via creative play, hands-on experience, seeing others practice critical skills, and one-on-one engagement. Because every kid is unique, you may choose the ideal strategies for your child's personality, age, and scenario.

Learning the social skills outlined in this book will give your kid the emotional intelligence necessary to be joyful and confident at home, on the playground, in the community, at school, and beyond!

FOR THE CHILD...

As you can see, there are two parts to these instructions. The second part of the introduction is dedicated to the child. The child needs to read or hear these words because they will encourage them and help them gain the required skills.

Making friends, listening, and speaking up in the best way possible is hard. I know, trust me, I have been there before. It might be discouraging to see everyone else making friends while you struggle. I understand!

My family traveled around a lot when I was a kid. I was continually at new schools, encircled by unknown people. I did not know how to make friends. I waited in vain, hoping someone would come to me and attempt to be my buddy.

I was frequently uneasy and alone. However, that is not going to be your tale. I wish someone had assisted me in developing my confidence. I wish someone had pushed me to make some risky decisions. I wish someone had taught me how to initiate and maintain conversations with strangers.

People with excellent social skills are not members of a closed club that you cannot join, despite how it may sometimes seem. You can improve your social abilities! I did not have this book then, but I finally learned how to improve my social skills.

I discovered what was holding me back and how to overcome my concerns. I even learned how to initiate conversations and, happily, form and maintain friendships. Fortunately, you will not have to wait as long as I did for your social skills! This book was created to teach you all of the social skills you will need right now to excel at school, at home, and in your community.

First, I will show you how to determine which abilities you currently have and which ones you wish to acquire. Then, I will teach you how to make and maintain friends and deal with all the bizarre things that might happen in between (when to inform others, how to deal with gossip, and much more).

What is more, the most enjoyable part? We will do it lighthearted, sometimes hilarious, since learning new skills should never be dull!

One thing to remember: you must read this book in chronological order. Have you ever attempted to construct a block tower? Isn't it true that one brick supports the other? The same theory applies to this book. I have listed more than 90 activities you may perform alone or with a family member.

You will also discover additional tasks to help you put your social abilities to the test in social settings. Each talent you master builds on the previous one. So do not miss any construction bricks in this book if you want your skyscraper to be robust and solid.

Do one action at a time before moving on to the next. Okay, one more thing: You cannot be a great ninja if you just practice ninja movements once a month, can you? You cannot rock your social skills until you practice them. Perfect practice makes perfect. So, remember to complete your exercises and practice the skills I teach you in each one.

Do you want to know who is incredible? You! Because you want to improve your social abilities and take a big step in the right direction. Let us get started!

1

WHAT ARE SOCIAL SKILLS AND WHY ARE THEY IMPORTANT

 This chapter presents us with one child's social skills. Through different explanations and examples, we will learn why social skills exist, what they are and represent, and why they are crucial for your kid.

We will start with their importance right now and then shift to their significance in the future. Also, you will be able to discover when some skills start developing, changing, and improving during childhood. This way, you will become capable of learning where your kid struggles and where they are in the developmental spectrum.

After discovering the benefits, you will learn the steps of modeling, teaching, and building social skills. For instance, you will learn how children find out about social skills in different familiar surroundings; easy step-by-step examples of how kids start conversations about social skills and new situations.

WHAT ARE SOCIAL SKILLS?

These are the actions and communication methods required to develop and sustain relationships successfully. Examples of social skills include initiating discussions, gaining friends, having excellent sportsmanship, and successfully dealing with bullying.

Social skills are one of the essential abilities that children and teenagers learn. They help them reach the highest level of success more quickly. Researchers from Pennsylvania State University and Duke University discovered that kids who scored better on social skills assessments were four times more likely to complete an undergraduate degree. These skills often help children acquire better job performance, well-being, and prosperity. In addition, those with adaptable social skills are frequently better at observing, problem-solving, and responding in social settings.

THE BENEFITS OF SOCIAL SKILLS

Helping children acquire social skills in childhood and at an early age may have a long-term impact on their health, happiness, and stability. Teachers, parents, and caregivers are accountable for building and improving the social ties of their students.

Children who lack social skills may find themselves in uncomfortable circumstances. For example, some children are in situations where they are unable to make new friends. These situations also include being unable to communicate, being unable to understand social conditions that may arise, having a poor understanding of jokes and figurative language, as well as when reading books, and being unable to cope with failure.

According to DiPerna and Elliot (2002), social skills aid students' reading and math success by affecting motivation, engagement, and study abilities.

Children who have acquired social skills are more likely to compete with other undesirable behaviors. It is critical to devel social solid skills to maintain a happy attitude and resolve difficulties that may emerge, such as bullying or hyperactivity.

Social skills assist teens in achieving better scholastic and employment achievements, more life success, and forming closer connections.

Antisocial behavior is becoming more infectious than compassion; fostering more socially acceptable behaviors is essential. The online education system may both benefit and hurt students. It heavily depends on the kid, their parents, instructors and tutors, and the school.

In short, the benefits of life social skills in children are:

- *Reduced Stress and Loneliness*

Children's social skills might help them cope with stress and loneliness. Children who can create and sustain connections are less likely to feel lonely. Furthermore, children feel less worried when they have trustworthy partners to whom they may turn for help when required. Research informs us that stress and loneliness are related to poor physical and mental health. That is why the development of social skills is even more critical. They promote good physical and psychological well-being.

- *Academic Achievement*

Academic performance connects to strong social skills. Thus, every child who can communicate has good social skills, performs well at school, and has good grades. The same child listens carefully, solves problems without issues, and can regulate emotions like a well-developed adult. Cooperative learning activities every day in schools attempt to provide students with real-world learning experiences that may boost academic performance. In these scenarios, children who can convey their thoughts to peers, listen to their peers' views with judgment, and then utilize this knowledge to create an assignment or project outperform those who fail to work well in a team.

Furthermore, when confronted with challenges in a group academic context, children who can self-regulate by being aware of emotions and employing effective and appropriate soothing measures may concentrate more quickly, wasting less educated time. Impulse control, or as we all know it, self-control, adds positiveness to academic performance because the kids with it have connections and listening skills that others without self-control lack.

- *Career Achievement*

While their careers may seem distant, time flies, and before you know it, your kid will be looking for weekend jobs or joining the workforce. Children with good social skills make great team members, caring coworkers, and responsible employees. Research supported by the Robert Wood Johnson Foundation investigated the social skills of over 700 kindergarten pupils before following their adult results.

The research found that actions associated with excellent social skills, such as sharing, resolving disagreements, and collaborating, may be linked to long-term success, such as obtaining higher schooling, finding higher-paying jobs, and feeling better mental health. Thanks to this research, we know that students rich in social skills can be fully employed later in life. Do you know why this is happening? Early social skill development may pave the way for solid social connectivity and meaningful participation in academic and social circumstances.

THE IMPACT OF UNDEVELOPED SOCIAL SKILLS

Children do not need to be social butterflies. Indeed, each kid will have unique personality characteristics that influence how they interact with others. Positive interactions, on the other hand, often help most people prosper. In addition, children and teens with strong social skills are more likely to grow confidence in their ability to approach situations and perform things effectively.

Parents must identify and assess any challenges their children may be experiencing. For example, peer rejection, harassment, conflict, isolation, despair, rage, anxiety, and poor academic achievement may all indicate a lack of social skills. That usually helps the kid feel better as well.

When social skills or interaction concerns go unaddressed, they may remain as a child grows up, becoming severe enough to substantially influence interaction, academic achievement, and even the capacity to join the job and prosper as an adult.

WHEN DO SOCIAL SKILLS DEVELOP?

From childhood to age, social skills are continually growing. We constantly get information from our surroundings, influencing how we respond in various circumstances or to specific individuals. We also often receive information from individuals around us, either verbally or nonverbally, about how our actions or words affect or might affect them.

Some vital social skills will emerge in your kid as they develop. Progress will vary from kid to child, as with other areas of child development. Some of these abilities may come sooner than anticipated, while others may appear later. That is usually no reason for worry, but always see your physician if you have concerns about your child's contacts, attitude, or health.

0 to 6 months
Social skills are already developing in infancy. Infants start making eye contact (a body language ability), smiling when they see familiar individuals, and laughing in response to fun actions.

6 to 12 months
Babies continue to acquire more eye contact and are better able to sustain this eye contact over the second part of the first year. They may also grin when approached socially by unfamiliar faces as well as familiar ones, replicate activities like clapping or pointing, reach toward caregivers, and react to others' facial expressions.

1 to 2 years
Toddlers begin to learn fundamental self-regulation abilities such as settling and calming down throughout their second year of life. That is also known as self-soothing. They may also start offering

toys to others and participate in role-playing activities such as replicating routines and behaviors. They also begin communicating vocally using essential words or phrases.

2 to 3 years

At this age, children learn to pretend activities such as cooking or cleaning the home at this age. They also learn to express their wishes or sentiments by asking for what they want and communicating assertively. They may also participate in caring activities, such as doll play, to demonstrate concern and awareness for the interests of others. This is when a child starts to play with another group of children.

3 to 4 years

Children in this age group continue to play with others, but they may now begin to play with classmates or siblings. This is the age where a child starts playing with other two or three kids. They may also act as though dolls and stuffed animals are alive and participate in social play with them. Children may begin expressing their emotions in several scenarios at this age. They may also show knowledge of family and society norms, particularly if they realize they have violated them! Children may also display spontaneous compassion and concern for others.

4 to 5 years

Children may participate in turn-taking and creative play with others throughout their fifth year of life. In their play, kids may be cooperating toward a shared objective, demonstrating early collaboration abilities. They begin to participate in creative space beyond their personal experiences, such as pretending to be a coffee shop barista. Children might enjoy games with basic rules, such as hide-and-seek or freeze dance. At this age, children are more talkative and participate in discussions with peers of the same age.

5 to 6 years

At this age, children may begin to participate in cooperative play with others with a common aim. Often, they imitate characters from their favorite cartoons, tv shows, or movies. Alternatively, they may be collaborating on a creative assignment, such as saving residents from a fire-breathing dragon! They may also start playing board games with adult supervision. The kids may even tell other children to be something ex: "I will be the princess while you be the dragon," etc. Children at this age usually can have more intelligent discussions with their classmates as they begin to inquire about other children's interests, experiences, and thoughts.

6-7 years old

Children continue to engage in peer play and may play in bigger groups. Often they will create games on their own and negotiate with others to make them play. They also play cooperative activities and are learning to deal with loss.

7-10 years old

In this part of their lives, their cognitive abilities improve a lot. They play with their classmates nonstop, collaborate with them, know how to implement their games, and also become more creative while playing. They play slowly but become competitive and goal-oriented because they understand many things. They also know how to cope.

Children are growing more conscious of other people's sentiments, views, and intentions. Interestingly, they now know that many emotions can coexist at once. They know, for example, that they might be thrilled about the big game yet be apprehensive about their performance. They show the capacity to cognitively absorb what they perceive in their surroundings and utilize this knowledge to take appropriate behaviors for themselves. As a result, they can think ahead and plan their activities.

For instance, if they wish to ask a buddy to participate, they may organize an activity ahead of time. When engaged in problem-solving activities, children of this age can better examine many parts of an issue at once.

Considerations That Can Affect Social Development

While social skills development typically follows these age groups, there will be variation among children, particularly those with disorders that impair social interaction. Engagement skills, communication, self-control, and other social abilities in children with autism may not develop as predicted. It is essential to mention that children who have ADHD do not often show self-control, emotion regulation, or age-appropriate abilities.

If your child has a disorder that affects their social relationships, development, or communication, consult with your physician to learn more about anticipated growth and ways to assist them individually and developmentally. The exercises in this book will be enjoyable for you and your kid! Discuss with your child's caregivers which areas (communication, mood management, etc.) should be prioritized right now, and then choose activities that emphasize those abilities.

HOW DO CHILDREN DEVELOP SOCIAL SKILLS?

The kids copy everything people around them do. That is a fact. Let us consider some particular cases.

- It is getting late in the afternoon. Nap time has finally come to an end. Dinner will not be ready for some time, but your kid is hungry. Your kid may notice how his siblings request snacks when hungry and utilize this example to acquire his food.
- When he watches a sibling ask, "Mom, may I please have a banana?" he can imitate the action and acquire food for himself. He may not ask so bluntly if he is a baby learning everything. However, he may make

noises to get what his brother has just obtained. Observing family members teaches newborns and children how to behave and gain the items they need in the home context.

- A huge queue in front of you during shopping. Your three-year-old kid is sitting in the shopping cart, looking around at the other people in line. This queue situation may be unfamiliar for your child, but looking at that particular queue and understanding what others do tells a lot. The child knows what patience is.
- Your kid notices others playing a game that seems fun at the park. She is unfamiliar with these kids and is puzzled about how to participate in the game. While watching them play, she may notice that others have joined the game. Observing how other children participate in the activity teaches her how she may also join in on the pleasure.

The critical work of navigating social circumstances like these consists of three fundamental steps: observing, thinking, and acting.

Step 1: Observation

Watching and noting crucial information falls under observation. Of course, this happens within the environment of the given child. Seeing may manifest itself in a variety of ways:

- Children watch what people are doing in their surroundings. They can also detect the mood of the surroundings. Is it a humorous, easygoing atmosphere, or do others seem serious?
- When children are in a new setting, they may watch the behavior of other children. What do the other children do? In which way do they complete their assignment? What are their strategies?
- Children are sensitive to other people's emotions. They may observe that a friend seems to be pleased to see them and then go to embrace the friend. Alternatively, kids may watch that a sibling appears dissatisfied with the game they are performing, prompting them to offer a new game.

Children use this knowledge to influence their activities, which directly affect others. For example, if the viewing or watch does not occur, children may select inappropriate actions or behaviors for the setting or scenario.

Step 2: Thinking

The second step, thinking, analyzes the seen information by considering what was observed and what knowledge may be used.

- What does it imply, for example, when I observe all the other kids sitting calmly on the carpet facing the teacher?

- What does it imply when my buddy sits alone and tears well up in her eyes?
- What does my mother's phone call at her workplace mean?

Thinking also entails understanding others' intentions, as in: What did he intend by that?

- What does the behavior indicate to me?

This talent develops through time, but it is a crucial piece of the jigsaw of social skill development. You may practice while out and about. For example, if your kid leaps in front of a buddy in line for the slide at the playground, their friend would almost certainly react negatively. "Hey, she cut in line!" the companion could exclaim. "It is not her turn! I was standing by."

Kids will absorb that social message over time: My pals are unhappy when I do not wait patiently and give them their fun. Others will gain from some adult supervision here. Take note of how your friend's face is frowning, with her arms crossed. What do you suppose she is thinking? What makes you believe she feels that way? What else could you do to make your friend feel better?

Step 3: Acting

After seeing and carefully considering information, children may behave in a manner that fits the setting (or does not!).

While younger children may skip forward to acting, completing all three parts of the procedure will result in a better end.

Children as young as 3-5 years old may begin to anticipate future results and plan their behaviors, such as getting closer to the bottom of the staircase before leaping off the last step, because they predict a painful bodily outcome if they jump off the top stage!

Young children can observe and learn from different situations. Consider this: "My sister cries when I pull her hair." This is a teachable moment, but how? By starting a conversation about the sister's feelings. Ask questions like "Do you want your sister to be unhappy?" if the answer is "No," continue with "Then, do not pull her hair." This age is a developmental age that can be used to initiate rational thinking and impulse control.

They are increasingly aware of how others are feeling and how their actions might affect those feelings at this stage. They may utilize the gathered knowledge, logically consider it, and then take appropriate action. While there are individual variances, many kids up to this age still perceive themselves as the center of their universe. They have difficulties viewing things from the viewpoint of others.

Helpful guidance for skill development is the thing your child needs!

When you find yourself in a scenario where your kid needs assistance addressing an issue, finding the appropriate words or the correct approach may be difficult. You may use the IDEAL technique proposed by the American Psychological Association to direct your discourse as you assist your kid through real-time problem-solving in social scenarios:

- Determine potential acceptable remedies by identifying the issue and the emotions involved in the circumstance.
- Consider each potential option.
- Take action after determining the best option.
- Experience is excellent for learning.

TIPS FOR HELPING KIDS

We have previously spoken about how you can aid your kid at the moment while they are in social settings. Additional strategies to create safe environments for your kid to acquire social skills are as follows:

- Give them plenty of practice chances! Join regular playgroups, be near neighbors, and go to the park.
- Play games together so kids can learn about taking turns and politely winning and losing. Hold informal

playdates so kids may learn to share and do what someone else wants.

- Video chat with friends or family to practice active listening and picking up on nonverbal clues in an electronic context.
- Teach your children how to recognize and label their own emotions and how to notice feelings in others.
- Teach empathy. Look for chances to discuss how others may be reacting. For example, show children how to envision how someone else could be dealing with emotions or with someone else's problems.
- Role-play before scenarios so the child may rehearse ahead of time. Practicing could help. Before reaching the park, practice a strategy by asking the question: "Can I join?" Before heading to art camp, role-play complementing a peer's work.
- Allow your child many possibilities for individual accomplishment and only intervene when required.
- Provide your child with a kind, supportive comments on social skills. Giving children various learning experiences while providing constructive, compassionate criticism and gentle direction will help them develop the critical social skills required for success in school, on the playground, and beyond.

2

COMMUNICATION SKILLS - SHALL WE TALK?

Kids begin communicating pretty early, from the minute they are born. For example, crying lets their mothers know something is wrong. Sometimes they even request something while crying.

Later, kids must learn to communicate to comprehend human society, present their thoughts to others, and grasp what knowledge others want to transmit (O'Neill. 2002).

Humans often communicate in three ways: verbally (via speech), nonverbally (through gestures), and visually. They include a variety of other abilities like listening, speaking, watching, and empathizing, so becoming a good communicator is not simple. Again, the role of parents and schools enters into play here. When you assist children develop excellent communication abilities at an early age, you immediately provide them with the necessary skill set for a successful future.

THE IMPORTANCE OF COMMUNICATION SKILLS IN A KID'S DEVELOPMENT

Having excellent communication skills helps us in many parts of life, both professional and personal. Communication skills may take a lifetime to perfect; thus, parents must start educating their children on how to communicate successfully from a young age to receive and share information effectively.

There are several reasons why children's communication abilities have grown more crucial in recent years:

- Children with good communication skills will be able to communicate effectively to get their thoughts through to others and be understood by others. However, it is equally critical that children learn how to speak successfully and appropriately communicate so they may respect and get respect.
- Communication skills may encourage the development of other essential abilities such as listening, speaking, watching, and sequencing, which is all crucial combination skill sets in children's development. A child who can communicate well

vocally seems to be good at making written communications, which may substantially assist him in achieving higher academic outcomes.

- Communication skills may impact your child's happiness since they will need to form social relationships with other individuals in this huge world. Children with strong communication skills may find establishing friends, connecting with classmates, sustaining relationships, and managing issues simpler.

- Kids with high communication skills may feel more at ease sharing their difficulties and expressing their thoughts; consequently, parents and instructors may get vocal signs from them that they need assistance. As a result, we can assist them in overcoming their challenges, improving their mental health, and treating behavioral disorders like depression, social disengagement, and poor self-esteem.

HOW TO DEVELOP COMMUNICATION SKILLS

As previously said, humans communicate in three ways: verbally (via speech), nonverbally (through gestures), and visually. Therefore, they must acquire all three communication abilities equally crucial to children throughout their lives.

Verbal communication is always essential since we must communicate effectively with other people to present the lecture topic, modify our language to the listener, and work well in a group (O'Neill. 2002). Children must learn to communicate correctly and effectively to be successful in life. Despite the company or job your children choose, being able to interact with employers, coworkers, and business partners will be critical in the future.

Second, nonverbal gestures are essential for kids to become effective communicators. Kids should learn to keep eye contact with the person they are chatting with to demonstrate that they are engaged in the discussion and respect the other person.

8 FUN ACTIVITIES TO IMPROVE COMMUNICATION

▷ **Activity #1**

Speak with the children as often as possible

Kids may learn a lot by mimicking their parents, and if parents communicate with their children regularly, their abilities will improve. Children who have difficulty communicating may be unwilling to speak at all.

The ultimate aim is for your children to feel comfortable starting and continuing the discussion with you. Therefore, parents and instructors must encourage their children to participate in the conversation as often as possible, to be patient in listening to them, and to ask pertinent questions.

Children may feel more comfortable expressing facts and opinions after participating in the discussion. In addition, there are several opportunities to converse with your children, such as when you all eat together as a family, go for a stroll in the park, drive your children home from school, or watch television together (O'Neill. 2002).

Remember to choose a relevant issue that your children are engaged in to be more open to communicating their opinions with you and encourage a meaningful sharing of information with others. Parents must pay attention to accurate pronunciation, grammar, and pace to talk correctly.

▷ **Activity #2**

Tell different types of stories.

Parents may share what they do and experience throughout the day and then invite their children to do the same to make it a regular habit. When parents and children are used to sharing their tales, it might be simpler to communicate when major concerns occur.

During the chat, parents may teach their children new words, correct grammatical problems, and encourage them to use intriguing phrases.

Parents may also play tale-telling games with their children by supplying them with colorful photos. For example, you might ask him to organize photographs in a logical order and create a tale out of them. Remember to participate in children's stories by asking questions such as, "What will happen next?" or "That is fantastic!" and "How could it have happened?"

▷ **Activity #3**

The whisper game

This popular and enjoyable game helps children improve their listening skills and is appropriate for children of all ages. You may also add other family members. Make a circle with everyone near enough to whisper easily. Begin with one child whispering a phrase into the ear of the kid sitting to the side, who then mouths it into the ears of his neighbor, and so on until everyone has had a turn. At the conclusion, the player reads the message aloud. Once completed, the last individual to receive it reveals the message. The initial message and the final delivered message are highly likely to change! Start simple and then include more complicated matters (O'Neill. 2002).

▷ **Activity #4**

Picture telling

Because children like telling tales, picture storytelling may be a fun pastime. Give your child a collection of images. Request that he organize them in a logical order and create a tale out of them. Alternatively, you may show him just one photo and ask him to describe what he sees in it, such as the landscape, people, colors, and other aspects.

▷ **Activity #5**

Presentation

This fun exercise will not only improve your child's spoken language abilities and help him become more comfortable in public. You may suggest various subjects, such as reciting a favorite poem or expressing his thoughts on contemporary issues such as water conservation, recycling, and the use of technology. Then, request that he prepare a brief presentation to give at a family gathering, a local park activity, or somewhere else he feels comfortable.

▷ **Activity #6**

Twenty Questions

Twenty questions is a great activity that helps your child develop the capacity to articulate and ask straightforward inquiries. Instruct the children to form a circle. Allow one child to stand in the center and think of a prominent location or personality. The other children in the group must identify it by answering 20 questions. The child may only react with yes or no. If the group fails to guess correctly, the child in the center is considered the winner!

▷ **Activity #7**

Teach kids about body gestures

Please establish adequate eye contact with your children while interacting with them. Parents must keep excellent eye contact with their children by sitting down and gazing at them. It is a method to make them feel at ease and express gratitude for their active engagement in the talk.

Nonverbal signals, often known as body language, may be complex for children who struggle with communication. Parents may teach their children how to use body language and explain its significance to them (O'Neill. 2002). You may say, "Mama is crossing my arms because I am upset," or "I feel insulted when you roll your eyes at me." Children may develop their communication abilities much more quickly and effectively this way.

▷ **Activity #8**

Emotional Charades

This enjoyable game is ideal for assisting children in understanding various facial expressions, gestures, and body postures while speaking. These are the nonverbal clues that supplement spoken communication. Give your child a few cards, each showing a different emotion or mood, such as anger, grief, boredom, weariness, or happiness, and have him play them out. Your children may also sketch the many feelings he is likely to feel in everyday settings.

Chapter summary:

Now that we have covered every important aspect of social life skills, their benefits, and a few tips and tricks, let us shift to the first necessary skill a child should obtain – listening.

3

LISTENING SKILLS - CAN YOU HEAR ME?

Listening is one of the key elements of language and communication and the primary vehicle for a child's learning, especially in the early years of school. Up to 80% of education (Johnson, 2020) in the early years is verbal, which is why we are so worried as practitioners when we encounter children with poor listening skills.

It is worth stopping for a minute to think about what we mean when we tell kids to listen. We are asking:

- Can you hear (Johnson, 2020) my voice?
- Can you hear the words I am saying?
- Can you stare at me or the item?

- Can you sort out background noise from other people chatting or natural noise?
- Can you see the sensory images?
- Can you break down my paragraphs and fully comprehend their meaning?
- Can you do this for a long time?

Many things are going on in this simple task. We ask children to participate in a complicated process that may be disturbed at any time by circumstances such as the child's developmental stage, cognitive capacity, mental condition, or health.

No one can develop listening skills in a short matter of time. It must be practiced and encouraged, just like any other talent. Explain the mechanism and developmental processes that may aid in developing these abilities and planning suitable activities.

THE ORIGIN OF SOUND; 3 SEPARATE PROCESSES

When kids "listen," they are using three separate processes:

▷ **Hearing**

The sense of hearing in a kid starts to emerge at a very early age. According to research, newborns can listen in the womb and react to their mother's voice within days after birth. Many children can understand and implement their hearing senses. However, just because a kid can hear us does not imply they are paying attention!

▷ Listening

Babies respond to noises, sounds, and voices (Johnson, 2020) at a very early age. For instance, a baby always reacts to voices. As children develop, they learn to distinguish between various sounds and recognize voices and noises in their environment. Kids gain the capacity to detect, discriminate, and recognize sounds, as well as interpret them (in words and sentences). These abilities are critical to the growth of speech, phonemic awareness, and, eventually, reading.

However, although children can hear and listen to noises and voices, they must also be able to focus on this "hearing" for extended periods.

▷ Attention

In the 1970s, psychotherapist Joan Reynell identified the several phases of attention that a kid would go through from birth to roughly the age of five as follows:

- Distractibility, 0–1 years: Infants have short attention spans and are readily distracted by unfamiliar noises or things.
- 1–2 years: Kids learn to concentrate their attention on one task and do not tolerate verbal or visual distractions. We have all talked to a child so

immersed in an activity (Johnson, 2020) that they do not seem to hear us.

- Single-channel focuses with more adaptability, 2–3 years: Kids continue to concentrate on one activity and struggle to transfer their focus when spoken to. Nonetheless, if their name is called (Johnson, 2020) or a visual diversion is presented, they begin to react to interruptions and diversions. Children still struggle to simultaneously focus on a visual and spoken job at this age.

- 3–4 years: children learn to manage their focus of attention (Johnson, 2020) and may move it between an activity and the presenter. Children must, however, continue to gaze at the person who speaks.

- 4–5 years: children may now shift their attention to a task and a speaker without pausing to look at them. Although their attention span remains limited, children are equipped to pay attention in a group setting. Children may now engage in both visual and linguistic activities simultaneously.

- Completely integrated focus, five years and up kids can now carry out a task, concentrate their attention in different sized groups, avoid distractions, and keep their attention for an extended period.

Not every child reacts to these phrases. As previously stated, several things might temporarily impair children's capacity to listen and attend.

THE IMPACT OF POOR LISTENING SKILLS

We can identify the child who has mastered these listening abilities. Our worry is for the children who have not, those who are "not listening," and these challenges may affect a kid in various ways.

▷ **Sound perception**

Children with weak hearing abilities will struggle to distinguish between sounds, such as the sounds human voices make or the noises other animals make. In addition, they may work to differentiate between diverse characteristics of sound, such as loudness or tone, which are the differences between an angry and a pleasant voice.

▷ **Reading comprehension and phonological awareness**

Children with weak listening skills (Johnson, 2020) will struggle to stay in groups for an extended time. Noisy situations will be too distracting for them. Listening to tales will be difficult, and they will quickly lose comprehension.

Another crucial part of the hearing is the capacity to discern between different sounds in words. They have to learn to spot the difference between syllables and phonemes. Recognizing such sounds will ultimately enable a child to mix and segment words.

These listening abilities are the foundation of phonological awareness, and a kid will battle to learn to read if they do not have them.

▷ Socializing and playing

Poor listening skills may significantly influence a child's life and education. Failure to concentrate and listen may lead to difficulty comprehending, following, and effectively completing activities. Often, this brings behavioral issues and low self-esteem.

Listening and attention issues might influence a child's play and ability to establish friends. A child who jumps from toy to toy is not participating in meaningful and excellent play that allows them to obtain significant experiences and information. If children are easily (Johnson, 2020) distracted, it will be difficult for them to participate in group play and reap the advantages of language growth and community skills.

▷ Communication and language

Developing underdeveloped listening skills may also influence a child's language and communication growth. For example, children may improve their vocabulary, understanding, and language abilities by listening to others (Johnson, 2020) and other people talking. These essential communication abilities serve as the foundation for reading and learning.

ENHANCING LISTENING ABILITIES

It may seem intimidating to listen and attend when confronted with struggling kids (Johnson, 2020). Nevertheless, numerous methods can aid in enhancing your children's listening skills, some of which you are probably currently doing without realizing it.

Active and Passive Listening

So, what if you are not actively listening? You may fall victim to passive listening. Passive listening means someone listens to something but does not try to understand it. Students that listen passively are easily diverted and do not remember knowledge.

Active listening encourages the listener to comprehend the speaker's message rather than just hearing a word they are speaking. Becoming a better listener is a talent that kids must actively cultivate and practice.

5 METHODS TO DEVELOP PROPER LISTENING SKILLS

Parents and instructors may model active listening for their children by becoming active listeners. Your kid will understand the value and significance of active listening if you demonstrate it to them. It also serves as a reference for your child when developing their listening habits.

Follow these five methods to improve your as well as your child's practical listening skills:

- Make eye contact

People who make eye contact demonstrate they are trust-worthy, friendly, gregarious, honest, confident, and energetic. Focusing your eyes may improve concentration. This allows you to comprehend what the speaker is saying ultimately.

- Please do not interrupt

Allow the speaker to finish their idea before responding. Do not interrupt, complete sentences for them, or hurry them. Avoid guessing or presuming where their ideas are going—this might hinder good communication.

- Pose questions

Asking specific questions is one method to demonstrate that you are listening (and to ensure that you hear accurately). This gives clarity, guarantees comprehension, and indicates that you are paying attention. Try asking the following four sorts of questions:

Open-ended: broaden the conversation

"How was your day at school today?" for example.

Closed-ended: ask for specifics

"Have you done your homework?"

Leading: encourages the responder to react in a specific manner.

"Do you have an excessive amount of homework?"

Reflective: broaden and extend one's thoughts

"You indicated in school that math is your favorite subject; tell me more about it."

- Re-tell what the speaker says

Use your own words to explain better what the speaker is saying. This confirms what other people are saying. Then, summarize the message by repeating the key ideas. In this way, you allow the other person to correct you when you are wrong.

- Look for the overall message

Any communication has two elements: the message's substance and the underlying sentiment or attitude. Both sections are critical to the message's significance. Pay attention to both the meaning and the underlying feelings. The actual news is sometimes found in the feeling rather than the information.

Following these suggestions will help you and your kid acquire the skills required to be more active listeners. In addition, practicing these procedures with your child can help them enhance their listening skills in the long run.

12 FUN ACTIVITIES TO IMPROVE LISTENING SKILLS

Listening activities that are active:

Teaching your child to be an engaged listener is simply the first step. It is also critical to put these talents into practice. Try these exercises to help your child enhance and grow their listening abilities.

- Tell your child tales. Inquire if they can forecast what would happen next. To create a sensible guess, your child must remember the details.
- Cook with your kid. Read the recipe and have your kid listen to and understand each step to ensure the dish is completed correctly.
- Talk about topics that your child is interested in. This allows your kid to participate in a genuine discussion and learn verbal communication skills.
- Play a game of telephone. Form a group and start whispering sentences to each other. Each individual repeats it until the last person. Have this individual speak the statement loudly and see how the two sentences differ.

- Write down a list of questions for your child. After one person has responded, check how many the other person can recall. Then, change roles and watch how the other person performs.
- Play the "spot the difference" game. Read a brief tale to your child. Then reread it while making modifications. Your child should raise a hand or applaud when they hear something that is not quite like before.

Use your imagination when it comes to "following the instructions." Give your kids brief, uncomplicated instructions and have them draw according to what they hear.

Additional games that might help improve abilities

Simon Says

A timeless classic that generations for a good cause have enjoyed! In case you forgot, one individual gives out directions that the remaining players must follow. Typical instructions include motions like 'place your hand on your head' or 'jump on one leg.' They will do it before the order. If they do not hear the phrase "Simon Says," they are out of the game.

The Whispering Game

This one is best performed in a group setting. It requires at least six players to succeed; therefore, this may be a fantastic game to start in a classroom or during a party. To begin, one individual whispers a statement to the next person. They must then whisper it to their neighbor, and so on until the message is spoken aloud by the final person. The first participant should write their statement so the other participants can see what they said.

It might be entertaining to switch who comes up with the initial statement and who is the last person to utter it aloud. You may also give the game a theme, such as telling them what they know about a specific topic if they have been studying it.

Musical Chairs

This is a terrific game to play at a celebration or in the classroom because of the more significant the number of players, the bigger the fun. Everyone begins by sitting on a chair, and the music starts playing. They have to stroll or dance while the chair is being removed. Of course, the last person remaining is eliminated if that person does not take a seat after the music ends.

Group Story

In this exercise, children learn to listen to others' ideas and be creative as part of a group. No one is directing them on what to do, but their contribution must be based on the previous person's concept. A narrative starts with one person stating one or two phrases, and then everyone takes turns continuing the story of the prior person's vision. The goal is not to say anything you want but to build on earlier remarks to create a cohesive tale.

Traffic Lights

Based on natural traffic lights, red indicates stop, and green means go in this game. It is more fun if you add additional colors and give them distinct movements, such as yellow walking like a crab and blue jumping jacks. The aim is for children to sprint to the finish and yells out the traffic signals. Start them with a green light, then stop them with a red light. Even more difficult is to say terms that correlate with the colors they are utilizing, like "screen light" or 'head-light.' If they do not listen, they should go back to the beginning. That will teach kids the necessity of paying close attention to what they are taught since failing to do so might have undesirable effects.

Sound search

So simple, but so effective! In this game, walk outside and have your child name all the noises they hear. You may visit a forest, a park, an industrial area, or a railroad station. Any location with a diversity of sounds is excellent. Do not assist; just ask kids what they hear. Active skills can be highly improved with this task.

Chapter summary:

Being a better listener needs a great deal of focus and dedication. However, active listening practices can help students develop communication skills and lifelong listening abilities. Now we will go on to the following chapter, which will teach us about body language.

4

BODY LANGUAGE - UNDERSTAND

 Nonverbal communication includes body language. The use of the body to communicate is known as body language. Besides animals, humans use this type of communication as well. However, some of this behavior is performed unconsciously (Korte, 2016). As a result, it differs from communicating through sign language, for instance. Body language is not used for communication, but sign language is.

Body posture, facial emotions, and eye movements are examples of body language behavior. In addition, body language can reveal information about a person's mood or state of mind. For example, it may signify anger, alertness, boredom, a calm condition, enjoyment, amusement, or drunkenness.

It is essential to company management, leadership, and settings where many people may see it. Also, it encourages interpersonal communication. It may also apply to certain people outside of the job. It is frequently beneficial in dating, mating, family environments, and parenting. Because body language is nonverbal or nonverbal communication, it may disclose a lot about your sentiments and meaning to others, as well as how others express their thoughts toward you. There are conscious and unconscious body language movements.

Positive body language may strengthen your bond with your kid. A smile, a nod, or eye contact can change a lot. Positive body language also aids child development since warm, caring interactions are essential for children's growth.

Positive body language is also vital for teaching your kid how to connect to and get along with others, which is a life skill. For example, using warm, loving body language with your kid might assist them in learning how to communicate affection. Likewise, pausing what you are doing to listen when your kid wants to speak teaches your child how to pay attention to others.

Negative body language tells a whole different story. It may not be true, but it could mean you do not want to communicate or spend time with your kid. If this occurs regularly, children may feel rejected or let down.

So to summarize:

POSITIVE BODY LANGUAGE

- Positive body language is a fairly dependable predictor of emotions. That is because it expresses attention to the other person and the discourse.
- Relaxed posture entails sitting comfortably, breathing slowly, and avoiding apparent rigidity or sudden movements.
- Uncrossed arms and open hands.
- Direct eye contact - Looking into another person's eyes, especially while speaking, shows interest in that person. To prevent staring, maintain proper eye contact by sometimes glancing away.
- Nodding - Using nods to punctuate significant points made by the other person indicate agreement, interest, and comprehension. Unconscious head bobbing suggests that the listener does not quite hear you.
- Taking notes suggests that there is participation and attention.
- Smiling and adding comedy - this is something quite positive. It suggests a friendly connection

- Leaning in - among two people, this tells that there is trust and positive feelings.
- Warm gestures - Talking with hands, especially with palms open, shows interest in the discussion and friendliness to the other person.

Moderation is the guideline for all of these friendly gestures. They might become more detrimental than good when overdone.

NEGATIVE BODY LANGUAGE

Negative body language is less dependable than positive body language as a predictor of a person's comfort level with the present discourse. Negative actions may just be a question of comfort for this person, a signal that the person is exhausted, or may stem from other problems hanging on this person's mind (Korte, 2016).

Tense muscles - stiffness, furrowed forehead, jerky bodily movement, hands clenched in front or down on the table might suggest apprehension about the subject or difficulty interacting with the other person.

- Arms folded in front - Forms a barrier and might convey opposition to what is being spoken.
- Hand on face - in many cases, this suggests boredom

- Moving about a lot, toying with items, and drumming fingertips are signs of boredom, anxiety, or agitation.
- Arms behind the head, reclining back - This might be a relaxing gesture in a well-established relationship.
- Yawning - definitely boredom
- Impatience - Attempting to disrupt what the other person says, repeatedly opening one's lips as if to interject.
- Eyes flickering, vacant glances, turning through literature without truly reading it, gazing at others in the workplace, and staring at the person's physique or clothes are all signs of distraction.
- Leaning away - It is very harmful to avoid approaching closer, even if something is delivered to the individual.

Negative facial expressions include shaking the head, narrowing the eyes, scowling, and frowning.

IMPROVING COMMUNICATION VIA BODY LANGUAGE AS WELL AS THE TONE OF VOICE

Body language relies heavily on body language and tone of voice. You may utilize them to deliver good nonverbal signals to your kid and to reinforce what you are saying to them.

Here are some suggestions for effective body language:

- Show attention by touching your kid's arm.
- Face your child and make plenty of eye contact. That means 'I am paying close attention to you' and 'You are significant to me.'
- Bring yourself down to your child's level. That demonstrates your desire to be close to your kid and make them feel safe. It also suggests improved eye contact.
- Employ your body language to demonstrate to your kid that you are attempting to comprehend their emotions. For instance, if your kid grins at you, return the smile. If your child is upset, bow your head and seem sad. Make eye contact and use a calm, soothing tone if your child seems agitated.
- When speaking with your kid, use a soothing tone of voice, a relaxed body posture, and a kind facial expression. This communicates that you are ready to listen. It also makes it simple for your child to understand when you are dissatisfied with their behavior.
- If your child enjoys cuddling, cuddle as much as possible!

IMPORTANCE OF POSITIVE BODY LANGUAGE IN CHILDREN

Presentation skills are crucial. To make their presence known in their home, school, and social life, our children, must learn to make a positive impression. Even the little motions people make unwittingly send a message to others. As parents, we must understand that a child's good body language can break down any challenging communication in life (Korte, 2016).

A positive body language plus posture stimulates brain cells and keeps you alert and energetic. In addition, it expands your lungs, allowing you to take in more oxygen. More oxygenated blood implies that the brain can perform more efficiently.

Retention and memory are significantly increased. Children will retain more of what they learn, improving their memory ability. Most significantly, it instills trust in children. So, let us look at how we can teach healthy body language skills to young children at a young age.

Children learn through their parents, neighbors, and instructors. Our children are, in the end, pretty similar to us. They are prone to replicate our habits, such as how we speak or move if we have them. The child will be wired to want their parents' affection and approval. They feel that if they imitate their parents, they will get their parents' love. Therefore, we need to be the first ones that develop good habits. In that way, we will teach our children what is right.

Whether reading an article or watching a movie, we must maintain proper posture. We may be standing or moving, but we must be conscious of our body language.

Parents must break some habits

- No smoking in front of your child.
- Make no unfavorable remarks about another individual in front of your kid to a member of your family.
- As a marriage, avoid needless conflicts.
- There should be no harsh language spoken in front of your child.
- No binge eating or drinking in front of your child.
- Never physically or verbally mistreat your kid.

IMPROVING FAMILY BODY LANGUAGE

Games, including family challenges, may be fun for your family to learn about body language. Here are some suggestions:

To help children tune in to body language, play guessing games. You may, for example, smile, nod, or adjust your facial expression to indicate how near an estimate is to the correct answer.

- Watch TV with mute. Observe your child. Try to figure out if they know what is going on without a single sound.
- Take turns practicing vocal tones during dinner, such as saying "I would like the salad please" in a surly tone and then in a kind tone.
- Draw images of faces with your child or play out emotions using toys. This may teach your child about how we frequently convey our sentiments without using words and how to recognize other people's feelings.

IMPROVING BODY LANGUAGE IN YOUR CHILD

Your kid learns about body language by seeing you and your body language. You may also assist your kid in different ways with body language.

For example, your kid may be standing near a friend, and the buddy may seem uneasy or begin to back away.

You may gently urge your child to give their buddy some space, saying something like, 'Anna, let us give Jack a little more room by taking a step back.' 'Well done, Jack has more room now.' You may praise your child if you see them performing what you have instructed them to do at another time. "Anna, I admire how you allowed Stacy some room to unwrap his gifts during the celebration,' for example.

Use body language to influence your child's behavior.

Body language may be helpful when distance or noise makes communication difficult. For example, when your kid receives an award at school or assists a buddy on the playground, you may offer them a grin and a "thumbs up."

Similarly, suppose you observe your kid misbehaving. In that case, you may use your facial expressions and body language to convey a message. For instance, shake your hand, raise it, or maybe use your head and shake it instead (Korte, 2016).

When your kid is misbehaving, you may utilize body language to emphasize your words. For example, try to stop and make your child listen by saying, "Annie, you are too hard on yourself. You can change that."

- Keeping continuous eye contact and speech tone.
- Lowering yourself to your child's level.
- If your child does not look up, grasp their hand to gain attention.

When your kid does or says something hilarious but undesirable, it may be challenging to match your nonverbal expression with your words. For instance, if a small child says, "Mom is a poo-head," or an older kid repeats something harsh an adult has said.

It is tempting to chuckle, yet doing so sends the wrong message. If your words and nonverbal cues coincide, your kid will likely grasp that this behavior is unacceptable. So, retain a straight face and a strong tone while saying something like, 'In our family, we talk to each other properly.'

CHILDREN WITH SPECIAL NEEDS

Those that have special needs, especially autism, may struggle a lot. They do not comprehend nor have the ability to communicate well, especially with body language.

Autistic children, for example, often need eye contact instruction. Do this by holding something your child loves in your hands. Continue doing this until your child looks up when they need something. Even though autistic children know how to make eye contact, they typically listen better when not staring at the speaker's eyes. Your communication style should vary because every child is different, and children do not act the same.

Some children have sensory sensitivity and may struggle with bodily contact, such as hugging. Other gestures of love or approbation may make these children feel more at ease. Consider the kind of body language your kid prefers and use it to convey approval, such as clapping, winking, or giving a thumbs-up (Korte, 2016).

10 FUN GAMES TO LEARN BODY LANGUAGE (FOR TEACHERS AND PARENTS)

Eye-Spot!

How adept are you at seeing little details? Identify the body language motions that help establish the character's personality by watching a brief video clip of any famous character. How do they express comfort and discomfort? Is their body language open or closed? Consider showing the video clip without sound and asking students to identify what they believe is described via the discussion. Following that, view the video clip with sound and evaluate your guesses. Are the movements and the words in sync?

Words Are Louder Than Actions

Your character has just gotten a letter from someone they have not heard from in a long time. Give the reader two words that describe what the letter says, and then spend the rest of the time explaining how the character responds while looking, rereading, and setting the letter down. Always pay close attention to their acts. Remember that the character's actions reveal more than words (Korte, 2016).

Your Character's View of the World

Teachers may use this exercise to include current events and/or themes that learners engage in other schools. This exercise may be done in two ways: as a writing task or as a role play. 1) People watch television when they learn about recent occurrences or issues. How do they react? 2) The character is transferred to that location and/or era. Describe what your character sees. Highlight the responses of the characters by their actions, conversation, and thoughts.

A Surprising Encounter

What would occur if two of the students met for the first time? Have two of them to the front of the room to act out their parts. Request that another student design a scenario where the characters might meet (church, party, red light, bus station). Secondly, have each kid spend 30 seconds introducing themselves to the class (Korte, 2016). Students will role-play for two minutes, concentrating on conversation and body expression. Discuss as a group if the conversation and body language felt appropriate for the characters.

A Catch-22 Situation

Allow each student to write out a "stuck circumstance" in which a character may find himself. For example, being pulled over by police, being informed they have three weeks to live, discovering they have magical abilities, etc. Gather the circumstances. Draw one scene and ask children to spend 5 minutes describing how their personality would respond to it at the start of each lesson. Start asking the students to identify what you are saying. This practice will assist students in getting to know their characters better and produce vignettes they can utilize as the foundation for a writing piece.

Charades

Playing games like charades, body language, and posture are essential to determining the correct response. It may teach your kid the significance of paying attention to others' body language. Including the whole family in body language reading will be a pleasant method without bringing attention to the learning side.

Investigating Posture

The participants take a tour around the room. Every half-minute or so, the game leader chooses a position the participants must adopt. They might, for instance, 'walk like a turtle' or "stand like a tree." Request that the participants pay attention to how the various positions make them feel. Following that, reflect on the postures by posing questions such as, "Which one made you feel the most scared?" or "which one probably makes you feel the strongest?"

Emotion recognition and facial expressions

Our facial expressions can convey much about what we think and feel (even unconsciously), so knowing how to interpret and portray them effectively is essential. According to research, children who can interpret the expressions of others are more likely to be deemed popular.

The Emotional Express

The Emotion Bus is an entertaining game for a small group of children. One child or adult serves as the bus driver and sits in front of the fictitious bus (use chairs, hoops, pillows, and clothes for the bus). The bus driver takes each passenger one at a time. Every passenger that buys a ticket and enters the bus feels a different emotion. Sometimes, some feelings are mimicked or adopted by others. For example, if a new passenger arrives weeping, all bus passengers will start crying. When all passengers are picked, they may be dropped off one by one, displaying emotion as they exit the bus (Korte, 2016).

Identify my feeling

To teach your kid how to interpret facial expressions, make flashcards with the most fundamental emotions: happy, sorrow, rage, fear, disgust, and surprise. You may then play a game in which one person must imagine a situation in which a person experiences this feeling. The other player can get points by accurately reproducing the expression on their face. For example, for the disgust card, player one may say, "Someone who just walked in dog poop." Then player two must correctly identify that it is disgust by making a disgusted expression. Once your child has mastered these fundamental emotions, you may make the game more challenging by including more complicated emotions such as envy, perplexity, pride, etc.

Chapter summary:

Nonverbal communication may be challenging to target with children of any age. However, children must employ nonverbal clues (face expressions, hand movements, and body language) to inform a buddy what to do to enhance their abilities. You may play nonverbal communication with your children so they can watch themselves using it. That makes it simpler to identify specific forms and comprehend how often we use nonverbal communication daily. Now, let us move on to the next chapter to learn about the significance of sharing and why it is so crucial for a child's growth (Korte, 2016).

5

SHARING - A STEP CLOSER TO ACCEPTANCE AND FRIENDLINESS

 Children must learn to share, establish and maintain friends, play peacefully, take turns, negotiate, and deal with disappointment (Sears, 2022). Sharing education encourages children to learn how to compromise and be fair. They understand that by sharing something small with others, there is a chance of getting what we desire after all.

Sharing is essential for other people, especially with children who engage in playdates or go to kindergarten or preschool.

THE IMPORTANCE OF SHARING - WHAT DO YOU HAVE TO DO?

Children may learn a lot by just observing what their parents do. When you model healthy sharing and turn-taking in your household, it sets a terrific example for your children to follow.

- Discuss why sharing is beneficial to your kid and others. For example, you may say, "If you share your toy or gadget, you could have more fun."
- Recognize excellent sharing with others. "Your buddy was sharing her toys pretty nicely," for example. "That was extremely thoughtful of her."
- When you see your child attempting to share or take turns, lavish them with praise and attention. "You did a great job with sharing today."
- Find and play games with your child that embrace sharing.

Before going on playdates with other children, talk with your kid about sharing. 'When Tila comes over, you will need to exchange some of your toys,' for example. 'Why don't we ask her what she would like to play with?' Before joining child care and preschool, you may also discuss sharing with your kid.

YOUR CHILD DOES NOT LIKE TO SHARE -
WHAT NOW?

If your kid has difficulty sharing, it is a good idea to be close while they play with other children and encourage them so they do not forget to share. Then, when sharing happens, do not hesitate, just praise your child and tell him what a great job he did (Sears, 2022).

Do not avoid playdates with other parents just because your child does not yet know how to share. Instead, use them to teach your child how to do it. Explain why it is crucial. It may assist in developing repercussions for not sharing for children over the age of three.

When using penalties for not sharing, ensure the repercussions are related to the object being shared – or not shared! For instance, if two toddlers do not share one toy, take the toy from both. The outcome will be the same for each child. This will also start a process of thinking. Your child will think about what went wrong and how to correct the behavior.

SHARING AT VARIOUS AGES

Toddlers

Your two-year-old is unlikely to comprehend the concept of sharing. The perfect case to describe this is a situation that involves two children that want the same thing or a situation in which your child does not have what the other one has. This is a teachable moment for sure. You must explain why waiting for something is crucial to your child.

Sharing also requires children to be able to regulate their emotions, something toddlers are just beginning to learn. As a result, your kid may attempt to grab the item they want or throw a tantrum if they cannot have it (Sears, 2022).

At this age, expecting your kid to be able to share is usually unreasonable. Keep in mind that restrictions do not work, but the guidance does. So support your child and practice it as much as possible.

Preschoolers

At three years old, a child understands sharing and role switching. You may help your preschooler develop their sharing abilities by observing and rewarding excellent turn-taking, supporting fairness, and explaining the concept of sharing. Activities that require sharing and taking turns, such as dressing up together or sketching a large image with the same package of crayons, might be beneficial (Sears, 2022).

If there is a problem, ask your preschooler how they would feel if someone removed their toy or did not allow them to have a turn. Talking to your kid about other people's emotions can also assist your child grasp things from another person's perspective.

Being realistic about a preschooler's capacity to share is a brilliant idea. However, most children at this age are still learning and may struggle to grasp the thoughts and feelings of others.

Children of school age

Most children comprehend that other individuals have emotions when they enter school. It tells us that sharing and taking turns is not a problem anymore. However, things could get complicated when a favorite object comes into play.

Your kid will be much more patient and tolerant at this age than they were before. Your kid will also be eager to do the right thing and will be able to build more complicated friendships. It will significantly aid with the concept of sharing. Sharing may also be practiced at school, for example, by sharing paints in art class or playing games together.

Sharing comes after selfishness.

Possession is a typical element of a child's developing understanding. During the initial three years, as the kid transitions from oneness to separation, this small person attempts to build a distinct identity from their mother. The stories in the toddler's newspaper shout, "I do it myself!" and "my!" In fact, "my" is one of the first words that a toddler will say.

A developing child develops bonds to both objects and people. Being emotionally healthy requires the capacity to create strong bonds. The one-year-old has trouble sharing her mother; the two-year-old has difficulty communicating with her teddy bear. Some children develop so devoted to a toy that the rumpled old doll becomes an extension of the kid (Sears, 2022). Hailey, four, would include her doll in her drawings of herself as if it were a part of her body. Can you think of a scenario in which she shares the doll? She could not feel safe and comfortable while the doll was in the hands of another child.

WHEN SHOULD YOU EXPECT YOUR KID TO SHARE?

True sharing requires empathy, the capacity to enter another's head and see things from their perspective. Children do not recognize compassion until they reach a certain age (in many cases, 6). Before that, they shared because you forced them. Expect a child under the age of two to be resistant to sharing. Parallel play is understandable for kids under two, but do not play with the children around them; they only play next to them. However, a selfish two-year-old may grow into a giving three or four-year-old with supervision and charity. Children learn the importance of sharing when they begin to interact with one another and collaborate in their play.

Children raised by attachment parents may be more sensitive to the needs of others and so more ready to share. They may be more conscious of their need to maintain their sense of self by avoiding giving. It is simpler to share with someone less strong or less dangerous than you (e.g., a guest rather than a brother, a placid kid rather than a demanding child). Your child's disposition determines much. When determining when your kid is ready to share, pay attention to his indications.

Expect limited sharing even at the age of four or five. A child may keep a few valuable belongings for himself. The child is unlikely to surrender her prized teddy or ragged blanket. Then, would you share your wedding ring, or the traditional shawl that was given to you by your mother? Respect and safeguard your child's right to own property.

Kids know other kids. Matthew assessed his buddy Johnny at the age of four, a reckless, curious boy who would have been an ideal durability test for a toy maker. Johnny investigated every moving mechanism, pulling and twisting them; only the most challenging toy could withstand this toddler (Sears, 2022). When Matthew noticed Johnny approaching, he knew his friend's destructive propensity and concealed his most precious and breakable items. We agreed with Matthew's insight.

Do not force it

Instead, foster attitudes and environments that encourage your child to share. Possession carries with it power. They are just toys to you, valued, and way too precious. Respect children's natural possessiveness while encouraging and modeling sharing. After that, start observing. The behavior is essential here. If he is always the victim, he must gain the ability to say "no." Many stages occur during the preschool years. For instance, your child will slowly but surely understand that the critical thing is to play with others and not alone.

Get in touch.

A kid provides just what he receives. For two reasons, children who experience attachment parenting during their first two years are likelier to become sharing children later in life. Children on the receiving side of charity (Sears, 2022) emulate their role models and become giving individuals themselves. Children that feel safe in the environments they are in really share more.

When teaching your kid to share, set a good example.

The monkey sees the monkey does. If a large monkey shares, a tiny monkey will as well. Make it a learning occasion when someone wants to borrow one of your "toys": "Mommy is sharing her recipes with her friend." Allow your generosity to show. "Would you want some of my popcorn?" ask your child. "Come sit with us; we will find you a seat." There may be moments when there is not enough of you to go around if you have numerous children, mainly if they are close in age. Two children cannot have one hundred percent of one parent. Do your utmost to split your time evenly. "It is not fair" may be childhood's most commonly heard complaint. Do not be afraid to be an equal parent.

When to intervene

Your children need to express their willingness to share. For example, "When Matilda is done with that toy, you could play with it," you say. "Please ask her when," or "Hold your turn; she will give it to you once she is done" When a toy dispute starts, it is best not to jump in and intervene. Also, allow your children to fix things on their own, between themselves, without drama.

Time-sharing

A timer might assist you in resolving toy squabbles. Johnny and Jimmy are fighting over the toy. Ask them to pick a number and then give it to the one with the lowest or the highest number. Set a timer right after. For a smaller child, two minutes is approximately correct. You may make older adults wait longer. Pass the toy right after.

It may take many cycles for a child to confidently give up the item, smiling because she knows she will receive it back. A family in our office who employs the timer approach informed us that it is so effective that the elder sister rushes to her mother and says, "Mom, set the timer." Connie refuses to share." Internally and externally, timers teach children essential life skills such as taking turns and delaying gratification.

If the time technique fails, time-out the toy. Put it somewhere else until children learn the rules. Children may whine for a time while the item lies unused. However, they will eventually realize it is better to share than lose the object entirely. They will find a compromise and collaborate so that everyone wins.

Prepare ahead of time.

If your kid has difficulty sharing his toys and playmate visits, ask the playmate's parent to bring toys. Toys that are unfamiliar to children are enticing. Your toddler will quickly discover that he needs to share his things to get his playmates. Bring toys if you are taking your sharing kid to the house of a non-sharing child. Many children have known about justice and fairness since being small.

Protect your child's interests while teaching them to share.

Respect your child's connection to his valuable items while encouraging him to share and be kind. A child's tendency to be greedy with certain toys and kind to others is typical. Protect the cherished toy. If the other child attempts to take it, pick it up. Make yourself the scapegoat. Make it easier for your child to share. Before play starts, have a chat with your child about sharable toys. "This is Susie's unique birthday toy," you may have to say. You may use these others until she is ready to share." Ownership should be respected.

The bigger the family, the more critical it is to balance valuing ownership and to encourage sharing. Children quickly grasp the notion of shared family toys, such as television.

Allow your child to express himself.

Janet handed four-year-old Benjamin an entire cookie with the plea, "Please give a portion of the biscuit to Robin," to promote sharing. He snatched it a bit and handed it to her. It was terrific practice for Benjamin, and two-year-old Robin learned about sharing from his example. Using older children as role models might help you teach principles to your younger children. In this scenario, both the instructor and the student learned a valuable lesson in values. Janet sighed a sigh of relief when Benjamin demonstrated the desired conduct.

13 FUN ACTIVITIES THAT IMPROVE THE SHARING PROCESS

<u>Toddlers</u>

Paint pictures together

Color or paint something with your child to teach them to share. Grab a big piece of white paper and your painting tools, then come up with a theme together. Do you want to paint a home or a flower? Then go to work, sharing your creative supplies as you go (Sears, 2022). Request the paintbrush. Share everything you know with them as well.

Play with the magic ball

This is a friendly game excellent for toddlers. It is also a fantastic way to teach kids to share. Kids move the ball from one to another as you sing the song's lyrics. No one wishes to hoard the ball in this game for fear of becoming "it!" Do you lack a ball? Play this game with an apple or an orange around the kitchen table! Do you know what to say?

A sharing song

Create a simple share song to sing with your kid, such as by playfully saying "Sharing is caring" repeatedly. You can also change the lyrics of some famous song or lullaby and make it about sharing by including essential words.

Distribute your focus.

Young children often struggle with sharing their attention. Let your children be around you while you teach about sharing. Engage with each of them independently. For example, play a game with your toddler, such as pat-a-cake, and then let him watch as you play tic-tac-toe with your other kid. Simply doing so teaches your child to share your attention.

Please pass the crackers.

Hand your child a handful of crackers. Request that they distribute one to each individual in the room. "Give your mother one," "Give your brother the other one." This may assist in regulating sharing for the children and teach them that it is a regular aspect of life.

Show them how to do it.

Use subtly demonstrated actions to explain how to share. When you share something with your child, make it clear that you are doing so. For example, you could say something like, "I will give you my pear." Here are some slices for you, as well as some for myself." When you lend a tool to a neighbor, tell your child that you share the nail scissors (Sears, 2022).

Concentrate on when your toddler gives and offers plenty of praise when he shares something with you throughout your usual play times, mainly when initially introducing this ability. Please do not make your child share; reward them when they do. Toddlers adore it when you seem thrilled when they do something nice, so be passionate about how wonderful it is when he shares.

Preschoolers

The Sharing Among Puppets game

When children are removed from the situation, they frequently comprehend the notion of sharing first. A solid emotional reaction happens when children do not get something they want. It is difficult to argue with them when they strongly desire something entirely for themselves. Puppets remove this emotional reaction, allowing children to view and think about sharing rationally.

This exercise requires at least two puppets. My favorite puppet I have ever had was a giant monkey. Here it is at work:

This monkey has provided many hours of entertainment and education. You will also need something to share amongst them, in addition to puppets. It might be as follows:

- Food for toys
- Pretend you are eating candy or chocolate.
- Toys, such as bears

Something like jewels or shells (such as these lovely shells on Amazon) or whatever else comes to mind. The following step explains how to exchange things between the two puppets.

The first thing is given to one puppet, while the second goes to the other. Continue this procedure. Then, check whether the children can replicate this method, evenly dividing the things amongst the two dolls one at a time. It is a terrific game for developing early counting, calculating abilities, and sharing.

The Monster Feeding game

A Monster is required for this game. Simply put, a container with a hole in it. You could make the creatures seem incredibly cool if you wanted, or you could keep it plain. So a lion, extraterrestrial, tiger, ghost, or anything else along those lines would be fantastic.

Then obtain something to feed the monster, such as dry spaghetti tubes. The concept is that each child takes turns putting a piece of 'meal' into the monster's mouth. Then comes the next kid, and so on.

Simple yet effective for taking turns and sharing the game. You could theoretically have two monsters, and the children could help distribute the food amongst them by feeding one, then maybe the second, and so on.

The Tambourine game

You need a circle made of children and instruments. Then, one child offers to sit in the center of the circle. They shut their eyes.

The kids start to pass the tambourine. After they get it, they shake it and then pass it away.

The adult will yell, 'Stop!' at any given time. Whoever has control of the tambourine will keep it motionless. The person in the circle's center will point to the person they believe is carrying the tambourine.

The Please Pass The Smile game

This is another basic 'passing' circle game. It is excellent for interpreting emotions, making eye contact, and communicating. After everyone forms a circle, the leading player (you) starts to smile at the first seen child. Then this child continues the process and smiles at the one next, and so on, and so on.

Complete the circle by passing the grin around. Keep in mind that other facial expressions are allowed as well. Next, give the balls around the ring. It is a pretty basic game that even small toddlers can play.

You will need a huge ball for this. Just sit around and pass the ball. If you want to make it more difficult, add a few balls to the mix and give them all around in the same order, several times around the circle.

The change game

This is how you expand on the previous basic ball pass game. It is now preferable to have two balls of various colors — for example, two blue balls and two red balls. My current favorite pick for this kind of exercise is a couple of packages of knobbly balls. These knobbly balls are ideal for sensory development.

Begin with one blue and one red ball. The blue ball is passed one way around the circle, while the red ball goes in the other direction. The challenging part is when the balls cross over each other. To make everything even more complicated, say, 'Change!' at any time. Then, the balls switch directions and return in the other direction.

Make it more challenging by adding extra balls, such as three going one direction (all blue) and three going the other (all red). Try yelling 'Change!' once they are up and running.

The Roll the Ball game

Get a huge rubber ball and set it towards the edge of the chute. Everyone stands up with their parachute. The goal is to roll the ball in a broad circle around the edge of the line, preventing it from sliding off. Can you complete a couple of parachute rotations? This game forces them to work together and share the chute.

The Competition for Rolling Balls game

This play is the challenging version of the 'Roll Ball' game if you want to add some competitiveness to your sharing experiences. Choose a line that runs through the center of the parachute, so everyone to the left of the parachute is on one team, whereas everyone to the right is on the other.

The aim is for members of one team to attempt to roll or bounce the ball off the chute on the opposing team's side. That team will aim to bounce it off the other team's side. Your team earns a point if you successfully bounce or toss the ball of your opponent's side. You might play first to three or first to five.

The Mushroom game

This is an excellent game for collaboration and sharing. Everyone stands up and forms a circle with the parachute. '1, 2, 3, Lift!' everybody says. Children raise the chute immediately, expanding into a giant mushroom. 'Mushroom Hide' is another option. This is similar, except that as you raise the chute, you all go forward and squat down. The parachute will form a large mushroom shape over the top of you.

Chapter summary:

Learning to share is a significant skill that some kids need years to master. It is lengthy, but some entertaining games, tools, and ideas can speed up the process. The next chapter will study self-control and being cool in various circumstances.

6

SELF-CONTROL - STAYING CALM

 Young children have a tough time dealing with painful emotions. Self-control and regulation are essential to instill in early childhood since a lack of self-control may have long-term consequences.

When children cannot engage in self-control, many negative consequences occur. Therefore, providing self-control skills via play and interactive activities is critical to helping a child's growth and capacity to deal with stressful circumstances (Coulson, 2017).

This article describes self-control in children and offers strategies to help young children develop self-control. There are also workbooks and activities to assist children in learning self-control strategies.

A DEFINITION OF SELF-CONTROL FOR CHILDREN

Before we can comprehend the concept of self-control, we must first understand the concept of the self. The word "self" indicates that it is the individual, not another person. Although "control" might link with a child who readily obeys adult commands, proper self-regulation is autonomous and self-initiated.

The ego-depletion model is a significant paradigm in the self-control literature. According to the ego-depletion model, self-control is based on a finite energy supply, and every effort to harness self-control depletes that energy.

On the other hand, the process model stresses that reaction patterns that emerge through time and our emotional responses are partially affected by the scenarios we choose from a set of possibilities.

The process model also highlights that emotions are primarily about valuation or deciding what is good for someone vs. negative for them. A valuation system consists of four pieces, which are listed below:

- Exposure to the outside world.
- Changes in the person's surroundings, both external and internal.

- The world's perception.
- What a person sees as occurring and how it seems to them.
- The world's evaluation.
- Whether their worldview is positive or negative.

People's desire to do action is based on their view of the world and desired condition. This model highlights self-control as a multi-step process with several cycles and iterations.

Children must have the opportunity to develop their vision of the world around them and comprehend how their aspirations intersect. However, it is also critical that they learn how to deal when these two notions do not align and how to maintain a healthy balance of their emotional reactions.

WHAT IS THE IMPORTANCE OF SELF-CONTROL?

Numerous research studies investigated the influence of self-control. Long-term success is dependent on children's capacity to manage their impulses. One of the most well-known studies tracked children for more than five decades.

The initial research gave preschool-aged children a marshmallow and told them that if they lasted 20 minutes, they would receive a larger snack. Sixty-seven percent of them were not able to resist. Following the exam, the children were tracked for almost five decades to see how self-control was associated with different life outcomes.

Children who resisted had more outstanding SAT scores, educational success, self-worth, and stress-coping abilities. Conversely, those with low self-regulation abilities have inferior health and behavioral outcomes. The years between the ages of six and 12 are critical for intervention and prevention since this age group is the most receptive to self-control tactics.

We will present you with techniques to assist kids of all ages develop self-control.

3 STRATEGIES FOR IMPROVING SELF-CONTROL

Because self-control requires planning, parents and care-givers must establish stability in a child's surroundings to encourage self-control tactics.

We have included some tips to help you help your child practice maintaining and fostering self-control.

Create a relaxing environment in which children may relax and concentrate.

Allowing children to take short pauses while working or participating in activities is an excellent method to help them develop self-control. When kids feel overwhelmed, having a designated spot in their bedroom or some other part of the home where they may do this is a fantastic approach to divert them.

When you see your kid is overloaded with emotions or acting out, encourage them to "go to their special spot." Engaging in calming tactics is an excellent way to assist with redirection. For example, allowing children to decorate their room and giving them stress-reduction techniques such as journaling, painting, and deep breathing are effective methods of helping them accept the space as a haven of serenity.

Provide children with appropriate options wherever feasible.

Everyone is required to accomplish duties that they do not wish to complete. Children will never enjoy every choice presented to them. Instead of giving children a firm "yes" or "no" answer when they ask questions, offer them some leeway, so they feel they have some say in the matter.

If they become able to exert influence, then they will feel safe. For example, offer alternatives if your kid struggles with food and does not always enjoy the meals you make. They can participate in making the decision rather than giving them an ultimatum regarding food or constantly giving in to their requests.

For example, suppose you are cooking chicken and veggies. In that case, you may offer the kid two ways to prepare the chicken or inquire which vegetables they like. They may take

out something from this circumstance and take responsibility.

Allow children to learn about self-control via play.

Several self-control games do not need much equipment. For
example, simple games like Simon Says, Red or Green Light,
and Freeze Tag are good for teaching toddlers about pausing
and considering their following actions.

Furthermore, offering children a diary to write down their
ideas rather than letting them out in more unpleasant ways
is an excellent method for helping them control. Giving children the chance to personalize the notebook (i.e., not
restricting the comments to writing) and enabling them to
draw pictures, compose poetry, or write tales about their
experiences gives a vital creative outlet to help children self-
regulate.

HOW PARENTS CAN HELP THEIR CHILDREN DEVELOPING SELF-CONTROL

Discuss important behaviors concisely and often. "Quiet
time is reading time." "Assign preferred toys to each other."
"Now is the moment to pay attention and follow instructions." "Helping others may make you and them happy."
Maintain basic norms and expectations, and remind kids
when it is time to obey them.

Create routines. Although young toddlers cannot distinguish time, they do develop acclimation to the rhythm of a routine. Active kids may be able to sit quietly while their teacher reads if they know that story time will be followed by outside play.

Make time during the day for cheerful movement. Recognize that young children have short attention spans by alternating calm, focused attention learning activities with chances for autonomous play and movement learning activities.

Draw attention to yourself quite often. The capacity to concentrate on learning activities is a critical executive function for future academic performance. Newborns are attracted to the most obvious stimuli in their surroundings. Infants learn to focus on specific cues highlighted by parents and caregivers throughout normal development.

Toddlers and preschoolers have almost limitless attention spans for things they like, such as constructing with blocks, making art, or playing favorite playground games. The challenge is to offer other educational activities that evoke the same degree of engagement. Reading with passion and excitement, creating engaging, hands-on instructional activities, and giving personalized attention and assistance to engage kids.

Make it into a game. Young children may benefit from computer games, including concentration-style card games, to help them strengthen their working memory. More active games, such as Red Light, Green Light, and Freeze, in which kids dance while music plays and freeze when it stops, need self-control from players.

During music class, the instructor might instruct pupils to play rhythm instruments or kazoos quickly or slowly in sync with a beat established by them. A broad range of games and activities allow kids to take control of their bodies, voices, and thoughts while they believe they are simply having fun.

Promote prosocial conduct. Learning to consider the emotions and well-being of others is another way to acquire self-control. Children engage more positively with their classmates as a result. Prosocial conduct is described as self-less interactions to assist others. Prosocial competence is an essential characteristic in and of itself, but it also corresponds with academic and social-emotional abilities.

Parents and early childhood educators may encourage young children to embrace prosocial behaviors by establishing clear expectations for sharing and assisting others regularly, modeling such activities themselves, and providing personalized, positive attention to each child. Instill the notion that when we serve others, we feel joyful, and they do.

Of course, young children, like all of us, have ups and downs. When young children get positive attention from loving people when they are sad or angry, they might realize they can control their emotions. Recognize when children are upset or excluded, speak with them about their emotions without dismissing them, and explore how they may deal with those feelings without harming others.

Building working memory in young children may help them transition from pre-reader to the reader. It improves their problem-solving skills by allowing them to keep crucial information in their brains while they compute responses.

Attending learning activities, remembering and following class rules, and positively connecting with classmates are additional parts of executive function. This boost the probability that children will thrive when they begin school and throughout their school years.

MEET MARCO

Marco is an 11-year-old child I once met who was so enthusiastic about the debut of a new video game that he would have traded a minor limb for it. So you can understand Marco's sadness when he discovered that he would not be able to purchase the game right away owing to the high price.

So Marco went into full "pester mode," convinced that his unwavering perseverance would finally wear his parents down and get him the prized game. Unfortunately, Marco was committing a standard error among children. Pestering him would not get him any closer to acquiring this game.

Marco never received the new video game, but he did learn some valuable lessons in its stead. Marco learned that nagging cost him the use of his existing video games. To his total surprise, he discovered that he could withstand the misery of not being able to get every new game that came out. Nobody expected it, but he also started to save money. This way, he had the money for Christmas, Easter, and birthdays and did not ask his parents to buy him games. Instead, he bought them for himself.

10 ENJOYABLE ACTIVITIES AND EXERCISES FOR CHILDREN TO ACQUIRE SELF-CONTROL

Tap the Balloon

This entertaining game requires just balloons and an open area. Arrange pupils in a circle and distribute them to two teams alternately (one child is team 1, the next child is team two, the next child is team one, and so forth). Make a circle out of balloons. "Team one!" exclaims the captain. Only team one students should tap the balloons (Coulson, 2017). Next, start with the second team. Finally, let team two tap the balloons. Switch on and off at 20-30 second intervals. Students will have to pay close attention to the audio signal that indicates it is their team's time to tap.

Want to include everyone in fun? Make use of colorful balloons. When the forbidden color is mentioned, do not touch the balloons. Then change the colors! Students must listen for the aural trigger and suppress urges when the forbidden hue appears nearby.

Jenga

Jenga's slow, deliberate motions are excellent for training self-control! If you move too quickly, the tower collapses. (Coulson, 2017). If you decide not to pay attention to the balance, be prepared for a tower collapse. Students will need to slow down and concentrate on the work at hand.

Breaking the Ice

Do not Break the Ice requires pupils to be highly conscious of their motions and learn body control, similar to Jenga. Excessive force might cause all of the ice to shatter! Use this with children who need additional time to learn how to be attentive to their bodies.

The Freeze Dance

This game requires no resources! Play music in an open area. While the music is playing, they will dance, but they will stop once the music is stopped! When pupils freeze, have them strike a yoga stance to add a layer of difficulty.

Green Light, Red Light

This is yet another game that requires no supplies! Every student stands on one side of the room. The adult in charge is on the other side of the area. With the phrase "green light," the students can start. Students must stop when the advisor, teacher, or parent says "red light." Change the needed actions to increase the challenge - pupils may hop, walk like a crab, or crawl on a green light!

The Garage Band

Each student will need an instrument for this exercise. Students will take turns becoming the leader of the garage band. The leader will establish the rhythm, and the other kids will follow it. Students must tune in and listen, then use body control to follow the rhythm.

Simon Says

Simon, or in this case you, or the child's teacher, says something like, "Touch your nose," but kids only obey the direction if it starts with, "Simon says." Children, for instance, would not touch their ears if Simon stated, "Touch your ear," but they would if Simon said, "Simon advises touch your ear."

Clapping Pattern

This is a great game to do as a group warm-up or to end a session. The counselor begins clapping in a sequence. All pupils follow the pattern, and then one kid adds to the practice. With the other additions, kids must follow the way. See how many variations you can make to the design!

Statue

The parent or teacher stands on one side of the room while the pupils stand on the other. The counselor turns away from the kids. The kids begin stealthily approaching the counselor. The counselor may turn around, but every kid must freeze in a statue pose and keep it until the parent or teacher turns around again! Anyone who moves is out of the game, according to the counselor.

Mirror

For this task, students should be paired up. The first student will be a mirror, while the other will be a person. The mirror student should duplicate the other student's motions, facial expressions, etcetera, precisely as if they were a mirror. They need to pay great attention and be conscious of their bodily motions!

Chapter summary:

Establishing a self-control exercise may not convert your children into Mr. or Ms. Olympia. However, it will make them develop into individuals who understand the importance of working hard, appreciating others, and finishing their job before watching the Bourne marathon. So, let us move on to the following chapter and study empathy.

7

EMPATHY SKILLS - I KNOW HOW YOU FEEL

Giving your children a new video game or smartphone may provide short-term enjoyment—okay, "little" is an understatement. On the other hand, seeing a favorite music singer in concert or attending the Super Bowl might be the experience of a lifetime. But what will it signify for their growth as human beings over time? What is the thing that the parents want for their kids?

You want them to become compassionate individuals who value long-term, meaningful partnerships and strong friendships (Trewa, 2020). You want kids to be self-sufficient and interact well with others. You want kids who not only rush to see their birthday gifts but also go to a homeless shelter or a children's hospital because there is a child somewhere whose parents could not buy toys for a holiday. You want your child to be a mensch, a Yiddish term meaning a decent person or soul. That is why we must educate empathy. It is a skill that will benefit you for the rest of your life.

This book's concept did not emerge from thin air. The present political climate has ripped our country's fabric in ways I have never seen before. Empathy is falling rapidly, paralleling a corresponding reduction in perspective-taking.

Acceptance of unique persons is dwindling. Various groups have been targeted at some point, whether it is Jewish tombstones being turned over, a Muslim girl's headscarf being snatched off her face, a Latinx kid being ordered to "go back to Mexico," or white people from a midwestern industrial town feeling as if no one cared when employment dried up.

The general public and the media neglect the children's pain. A problem that nobody mentions. Trolling and cyberbullying are new terms in our lexicon, but the effects of online abuse may be just as damaging as in-person abuse. For example, Tyler Clementi, an eighteen-year-old Rutgers College student with his entire life in front of him, committed suicide in 2010 by jumping off the George Washington Bridge between New York and New Jersey. After being humiliated online by his flatmate, who secretly taped him via webcam and distributed the video on Twitter for chuckles.

One person with empathy, one college student who stood by him, may have saved his life. Nobody wants to be the "other." Nobody likes to be an outsider or feel insignificant. However, this happens sooner or later regardless of whether we want it.

As adults, we are inundated with parenting books and advice and are unsure which aspect to prioritize first. Is it tough? Angela Duckworth, a New York Times best-selling author, authored a book (Trewa, 2020) on grit and its role in primary education. Is it tough? Dr. Kenneth R. Ginsburg is the authority in teaching children resilience.

However, I believe parents and teachers should prioritize guiding our children to develop empathy. After laying that foundation, we may add additional building stones such as honesty, tolerance, respect, understanding for variety, and empowerment (also known as empathic action) to produce winning, sentient, and successful humans.

Empathy is more important than ever. We cannot have compassion if we do not engage with one another. It is practically difficult if we are preoccupied with ourselves at the expense of others. However, it is on the decline when we need it the most. Screens are one of the main offenders. If children are staring at screens, they are not engaging with human faces; if they believe they are, they are delusory.

How often have you summoned your kid for supper to find them still playing Candy Crush or chatting on Instagram with a buddy five minutes later? How often have your children begun Googling something during meals because it was "essential," only to find out it was something trivial, such as the lyrics to a song they could not remember? How many "urgent" phone calls should a middle schooler take during dinner?

There are several reasons why parents should prioritize instilling empathy and emotional intelligence in their children. Empathy means putting yourself in someone else's shoes to understand their situation and side.

WHY EMOTIONAL INTELLIGENCE AND EMPATHY ARE IMPORTANT

Empathy is a valuable life skill, according to research. Therefore, emotional intelligence and emotional quotient (E.Q.) is thought to be more essential to success than I.Q., or intelligence quotient. Emotional intelligence and emotional quotient (E.Q.) is defined as being able to comprehend one's feelings and the feelings of others, as well as being able to regulate one's own emotions and exercise self-control.

According to research (and for kids in school), empathy is vital for developing healthy and happy connections with family and friends and doing well at work, according to research (and with kids in school). So it makes sense—after all, whom would you like to work with: someone who is friendly, attentive, and courteous, or who has no respect for your opinions or feelings?

Empathy may also help teach children what bullying is and how not to participate in bullying behavior. Thus, teaching empathy is a critical basis for reducing bullying in schools.

THE ADVANTAGES OF EMOTIONAL INTELLIGENCE

Several decades of research have shown that emotional intelligence delivers many advantages that will benefit your kid for the rest of her life. Emotional intelligence can be helpful, and here is how:

On standardized examinations, children with greater levels of emotional intelligence do better. They also have better grade point averages. That is because E.Q. links with I.Q. - both at their highest levels, of course.

Improved connections. Emotional intelligence abilities assist children in managing conflict and developing stronger bonds. Adults with more significant emotional intelligence report having stronger personal and professional relationships.

E.Q. during childhood is linked with more outstanding adult achievement. 19-year research discovered that a kindergarten child's physical and mental abilities might predict long-term success. Kids that can collaborate and simultaneously share plus follow instructions up to the age of five are more likely to get a college degree and begin working full-time by 25.

Mental health is another improved thing. Individuals who are extremely emotionally intelligent do not suffer from mental diseases as often.

The advantages of emotional intelligence are apparent. Children who can control their emotions when upset is more likely to succeed in challenging situations. Furthermore, a kid who can healthily show their feelings is more likely to have good connections than a child who yells or says hurtful things when they are furious.

It has been said that children do not always kids can gain emotional intelligence abilities. So why not all of them have it? Because adults do not always show or know how to show them.

HOW PARENTS CAN HELP THEIR CHILDREN DEVELOP EMOTIONAL INTELLIGENCE AND EMPATHY

Make sure that your child's emotional needs are satisfied. To be able to feel and show sympathy for someone else, a child's feelings and needs must first be satisfied. Before providing it to others, she must rely on her parents and caretakers for comfort and support.

Teach your kid how to deal with difficult emotions. For example, rage, together with envy, are normal to express during a lifetime. However, a kid taught by sympathetic parents how to deal with these emotions in a constructive, problem-solving manner is more likely to develop significant emotional intelligence and empathy.

"How would you feel?" you should ask. Children are predisposed to empathize. When toddlers observe someone in evident emotional anguish, they are likely to sympathize and attempt to console that person. At the same time, young toddlers are naturally self-centered. When a preschooler slaps a sibling or a friend or takes away an item they are playing with; a parent must explain that such action might cause physical or emotional harm to another person. "How would you feel when someone took your toy away from you?" or "How would you feel if someone struck you?"

Name that sensation. Identify and categorize emotions and feelings as much as possible to assist your kid in comprehending them. For example, if your kid is kind to someone, say something like, "That was good of you to be so concerned about your buddy; I am sure it helped him feel much better when you were so kind to him." If your kid acts cruelly or negatively, tell him, "I know you are furious, but you made your buddy unhappy when you grabbed his toy."

Discuss both good and bad behavior in your environment. In real life, books, television, and movies expose us to instances of good and poor conduct. Discuss with your kid any inappropriate behavior you see, such as someone causing another person upset or behaving like a bully or someone helping others and making others feel good about themselves.

Discuss the many forms of conduct and their consequences.

Lead by example. Your kid observes you and other adults in her life to learn how to connect with others. Demonstrate to her what it is to be philanthropic or kind and compassionate. You will teach your kid empathy through assisting family members and neighbors, as well as supporting friends and those in need or going through a difficult period.

HOW TO TEACH HEALTHY COPING STRATEGIES

When kids start to understand their feelings, they must learn how to cope with them healthily. But unfortunately, it may be difficult for children to know how to relax, cheer themselves up, or confront their concerns.

Teach certain abilities. For instance, when your kid is furious, they may benefit from understanding and taking a few deep breaths to calm their body down. A kid-friendly technique to teach this is to have them do "bubble breaths." During this activity, they breathe in and throw bubbles with their nose or mouth.

You might also help your kid develop a kit to control their emotions. Coloring books, beloved joke books, relaxing music, and scented lotions are a few examples of goods that might enhance their senses and soothe their feelings. First, place the things in a specially decorated box. Then, when they are agitated, tell them to collect their calm down kit and practice using their skills to regulate their emotions.

Make Emotional Intelligence a Lifelong Objective

No matter how emotionally educated your kid seems, there is always space for growth. Furthermore, there will undoubtedly be ups and downs during childhood and youth. In addition, they are likely to experience hurdles that will test their abilities as they age. So make it a mission to include skill development into your daily life. Talk about emotions with your kid daily while they are young.

Discuss the feelings that characters in novels or movies may be experiencing. Discuss better methods to address difficulties or tactics characters may employ to treat people respectfully.

As your kid ages, discuss real-life issues with them, whether they are something they face in their everyday lives or a topic you read about in the news. Make it a continuous discussion.

Use your child's errors to help him, or her develop. For example, when they act out since they are upset or have been damaged by someone's emotions, take the opportunity to discuss how they might improve in the future. Your kid may acquire the emotional intelligence and mental power required for success in life with your continued support and direction.

A success story

As early as preschool, children in the Danish education system engage in a nationwide Step by Step program. The youngsters are shown photographs of children expressing various emotions such as grief, fear, impatience, and delight. The pupils discuss what they observe and articulate how the other youngster feels. They learn empathy and how to interpret facial emotions using this way. Facilitators and other observers are not judgemental and help the youngsters feel comfortable.
CAT-kit, another popular software, aims to improve emotional awareness and empathy. It employs instruments such as face image cards, measuring sticks to assess emotional intensity, and body pictures on which participants may sketch emotions' physical elements and location. Children may use the application to explain their experiences, ideas, feelings, and sensations.
Most parents in Denmark do not criticize other children in front of their children. They are always looking for methods to help their children comprehend another child's behavior without labeling it negatively. Remembering that all children are innately good enables us, parents, to model goodness in others.
Well-known writers Jessica Alexander and Iben Dissing Sandahl give three essential pieces of advice for parents to foster happy, well-adjusted children in their book The Danish Way of Parenting:

What the Happiest People in the World Know about Raising
Confident, Capable Kids:
Read to kids a variety of tales, not only joyful ones. Reading about
challenging emotions may be an excellent method of developing
empathy. The issues included in many Danish children's books are
frightening by American standards, but studies have shown that
reading about all emotions strengthens a child's capacity to empathize.
The original Little Mermaid, a Danish myth, does not win the
prince and instead dies of despair and dissolves into sea foam. That
brings up a whole other line of thought! Books are an excellent tool
for teaching empathy.

9 AGE-APPROPRIATE EXERCISES AND ACTIVITIES

Here are some age-appropriate practices for helping kids develop empathy. Start with a few exercises or ideas that you believe may appeal to your child, based on the age groups listed below. Some activities taught to younger children may continue into adulthood.

▷ 3 to 5 years

Describe and label the situation

Help youngsters notice their own and others' feelings by describing and categorizing them (for example, "You appear furious," or "Are you sad?"). You can also encourage body awareness since young children may find it simpler to recognize emotions based on how their bodies feel.

"You are clenching your fists," you can say, for example. You made a stomping sound with your feet. "You appear to be upset." Children will detect and analyze the feelings of others as they become more conscious of their own emotions (Trewa, 2020).

Storytelling

As you read stories to your child, inquire about the characters' feelings in the stories. From our collection of activities and stories to teach empathy to kids, here is one example:

Gabi Garcia's story "Listening with My Heart" is about Esperanza, who tries to be compassionate to herself and others when situations do not go as planned (Trewa, 2020). Questions and activities about empathy can be found in Gabi Garcia's free discussion and activity guide. Ask questions such as:

- What does Esperanza think at the start of the story? What changes in Esperanza's feelings during the story?
- What does Bao think at the beginning? What affects Bao's emotions?
- When Esperanza fled off the stage, how did she feel?
- If you could, what would you say to Esperanza?
- If this happened to you, how would you react?
- What does Esperanza do to make herself a good friend?
- How can a person become better as a friend?

You might also read and discuss how it seems when others are cruel in Kevin Henkes' novel *Chrysanthemum*, where Chrysanthemum adores her unusual name—until others begin to ridicule her about it.

Drew Daywalt's *The Day the Crayons Quit* is another excellent book for explaining emotions with young children. Duncan just wishes to color in this vibrant story. His crayons, sadly, are on strike. Beige is disregarded in favor of brown, black is only used for outlines, orange and yellow are at odds over whether a color is the actual sun color, etcetera.

You can also name the shades and label them as feelings. This is also a fantastic method to explain that everyone has different wants, hopes, and goals and that finding solutions for everyone to agree on might be difficult. You can use a similar strategy with any story that your kids enjoy!

A "We care" center

A basic box with Band-Aids, or maybe Kleenex, and a small plush animal can serve as a We Care Center. It serves as a symbolic tool for youngsters to express empathy for others who are suffering. A young child, for example, might detect that Mom is sad—or simply sneezing—and give tissues. This encourages youngsters to be aware of their surroundings and to recognize that our reactions and actions can have a beneficial impact.

"Our friends are sick" can be used to model this connection. Let us go get them some soup to cheer them up!" "Your brother injured his elbow," for example. Let us lend a hand and bring him a Band-Aid!"

Work on social skills right now.

If your kid takes something that does not belong to it, feel free to ask, "How does the person whose toy belongs to it feel?" When your sibling takes your toys, how do you feel? Take a look at his features. He appears to be depressed (Trewa, 2020). Instead of stealing your brother's toy, what else could we do?"

You might teach a more acceptable response to want a toy at this point, such as asking for a turn, negotiating a trade, or waiting with some other toy. When children learn social skills in context, it is much easier to understand them.

▷ 5-7 years old

Play emotion charades

Empathy in kids can be developed by teaching emotions through play. Children can learn the vocabulary to express and comprehend sentiments through games and activities. Take turns playing out emotions and identifying the feelings in this game of emotion charades. You can talk about the emotion after a player has guessed correctly by asking questions like:

- When do you get depressed?
- What helps you feel better when you are upset?

- What can we do to aid someone who is depressed?

A helpful version of this game is suggested all over the internet. She represents many emotions using characters from the film Inside Out. She cuts out the characters' photos and glues them to index cards. The actor then acts out that emotion by drawing an index card from a bucket. The other kids estimate the feeling by holding the relevant Inside Out character figurine.

Make use of images

Another excellent technique to assist children in learning is to use visual aids. For example, cut out magazines and print photos from the internet that portray sad, angry, or joyful faces if your youngster has problems recognizing and/or categorizing emotions. You can also progress to more complicated emotions such as fear, embarrassment, disappointment, frustration, etcetera.

You might question youngsters about instances when they felt the same way as the people in the photographs while you talk about how they feel. Include personal examples to demonstrate that even grownups struggle with strong emotions and that this is entirely acceptable.

Accept and value differences.

Respect for others from various backgrounds is a crucial component of empathy. "It can be difficult for children to understand the connection between how they feel when something happens and how another person would feel about the same thing." Furthermore, it is even more complicated when the other person looks or acts differently than they do."

Allow your child to interact with youngsters of other races, backgrounds, abilities, sexes, etcetera. You can also read literature or watch television programs about children not your child's age. Assist kids in recognizing and focusing on what they have in connection with others.

Pay attention to what others are doing.

Play a game where you study other people in a crowded public setting, such as a park, to help your youngster understand nonverbal clues. Take note of other people's body language and make educated guesses about how they are feeling. For example, "That child's head is drooping, and his shoulders are slumped." "He appears to be depressed, in my opinion." "I am curious as to why he feels that way."

Set appropriate limits and boundaries for your children

As children age, they must learn that empathy does not imply taking on everyone else's issues and wants. It does not mean you should always say "yes" or drop everything to aid others.

Follow these three steps to teach your children to recognize and respect their needs.

Make a plan for how your child will react in different situations. For example, if another child provides an unwelcome embrace, your kid can respond, "I do not like that." "Please do not come near me." "My name is _____," your youngster can say if a child calls him or her by that name. Instead, call me that."

Make a list of situations in which you will need to seek adult assistance, such as a youngster who will not accept no for an answer or any circumstance that feels hazardous or unpleasant. Also, clarify that helping others should not entail breaking laws or doing something your child does not want to do.

Respect your child's personal space. Do not force the issue if your youngster does not enjoy being tickled or scooped up and whirled around. "I understand," you say. I am not going to do that again." When your kid says "no," this is how they should expect others to respond.

▷ 7-9 **Years**

Read more advanced literature and discuss the characters' thoughts, beliefs, desires, and feelings in-depth. What evidence do we have?

Read Trudy Ludwig's *The Invisible Kid*, for instance, in which a little boy named Brian battles with the feeling of being invisible. He is never asked to any parties and games. Brian is the first person to greet a new pupil. After working together on a class project, Brain starts to shine. The book teaches kids that tiny acts of kindness can make them feel included and help them thrive. After you have finished reading, consider the following questions:

- Why did Brian feel as though he was invisible?
- What do you suppose it is like for Brian to be "invisible?"
- What did Brian do to make Justin feel at ease?
- How did Justin assist Brian in becoming more "visible?"
- Have you ever felt excluded or unnoticed? What would have made you feel more visible or included?

In one study, 110 elementary school students (aged seven) engaged in a reading program. Some students were given the task of having discussions about the emotional impact of the stories they read at random. Others were merely required to create drawings based on the narrative.

The kids in the dialogue group made more progress in emotional understanding, theory of mind, and compassion after two months, and the good outcomes "stayed steady for six months."

You might choose books closely applicable to empathy to read with your children. Alternatively, pay attention to what your kids are reading and involve them in discussions about the characters, their feelings, and what they may think, feel, or do in similar circumstances.

Meditation on loving-kindness and compassion

According to research, as little as two days of training in kindness and compassion meditations can result in changes in brain chemistry associated with an improvement in beneficial social behaviors, such as empathy. In addition to enhanced health, these meditations result in greater happy feelings and social connectedness.

Kindness with love Meditation entails thinking and sending happy thoughts to loved ones. Later on, your child can broaden her positive thinking to include more neutral persons in her life.

"May you feel protected" is one of the four standard phrases for this meditation. May you be content. May you be in good health. "May you have a happy life." It does not matter how you and your child say it; what matters is that you and your child generate feelings of love and warmth.

Children who have received compassion training picture sad or upsetting experiences related to them with warmth and care. They then repeat the practice with other people, first with close friends and family, then a difficult person, and lastly humanity as a whole.

Play cooperative board games or work together to build something

According to research, practical collaborative experiences motivate us to collaborate more in the future. Working with others can enable kids to form healthy relationships and be receptive to more in the future.

These encounters can include discussions and debates, encouraging children to examine different points of view. The following are some suggestions for cooperative games or collaborative construction:

- Play with Legos and collaborate to create something specific.
- It is a Treasure Hunt! (a game where children run in places to find something).
- Outfoxed! (a game in which players work together to solve a mystery).
- Soup with Stones (a cooperative matching game that includes awards).
- The Secret Door (a board game in which children aged five and up collaborate to unravel the mystery behind doors).

Since empathy is such a big deal in a child's development, we have included extra content for over nine years to help you in the future and ensure you remain on the right track while engaging with your child. This part is perfect for teachers, counselors, and educators.

▷ **9 to 11 years old**

Enroll in acting classes

Get your kid interested in theater as well as acting classes if he is interested. Playing pretend assists young people learn compassion and understanding for others, and assuming another person's position is a terrific method to develop empathy.

Make an empathy map

Do, think, feel, and say are the four sections of an empathy map. First, choose an emotion, then consider what you may say, think, or do when you are experiencing that emotion. "When I am scared, I may believe I am making many errors or that something horrible is going to happen," for instance.

You can also mention that people think something and act the opposite of it. Finally, you can talk about why this occurs and how it relates to understanding and empathy for others.

▷ **Ages 12 and up**

Talk about current events.

By reading the paper, magazine articles, or watching the news together, you can learn about current events and develop empathy. Use this in everyday situations as well, right after your child mentions something happening at the moment.

Pose queries such as

- What are the emotions of those concerned in this situation?
- In a similar situation, how would you react?
- Is there anything else we can do to assist you?

Encourage your kid to participate in community service

Encourage your kid to participate in volunteer activities that they enjoy. As children age, they can play a more direct part in assisting their community or society. They may even choose to start their projects or philanthropic organizations to address a problem that they are passionate about.

Observe the line

This game is ideal for classrooms, summer programs, or other settings when a large group of older kids is present. For example, the phrase "Walk the Line" was displayed in the film Freedom Writers.

Place a ribbon line in the center of the room, with pupils facing the lines on both sides. Read through a list of statements. If the student agrees with the information, they should proceed to the front of the queue. "I have lost a relative," "I have been picked on at school," etcetera, are examples of such remarks. Students can also assist in the creation of the prompts.

The activity demonstrates their shared problems and helps them comprehend what their classmates are going through and feeling. Finally, students come to their seats after the session to reflect via writing or conversation.

One alternative is to have students send a letter to a kid who stepped to the line on one of the same triggers, revealing more about their experience or encouraging them.

What is next? Learning and conquering problem-solving skills!

8

PROBLEM-SOLVING SKILLS - I CAN FIX THAT!

 Problem-solving skills are different in each child. Some have them; some do not. The problems start to surface when they go to school or face a difficult situation at home. Problem-solving approaches are good for them because, in this way, they will be prepared for the upcoming obstacles and issues in both their academic and personal life (Morin, 2022).

Experts agree that confidence in facing obstacles is "an essential characteristic for school preparedness." As we mentioned in the chapters above, children learn by observing others. We face challenges regularly, whether at school or home, but it is part of our routine to fix them and go on.

For a youngster, however, this is a vital life skill to master to make healthy choices for themselves. If a child can solve difficulties on their own, they will be happier, more confident, and independent; they will not be irritated or discouraged by their inefficiency. This is why we must begin teaching problem-solving abilities to children at a young age.

Rather than being seen negatively, problems contribute to developing character, resilience, and tenacity. They allow us to see and perform things differently and elicit lateral thinking. For example, when faced with difficulty, a child who lacks problem-solving abilities may avoid trying something new, dismiss certain situations entirely, or act rashly.

Children, like adults, confront challenges daily; rather than jumping to their aid, allow your youngster to try to solve the situation independently. Keep an eye on how they study and approach the problem and communicate about it to find a solution together. Then, when your child has a similar challenge in the future, they will be able to draw on and employ these tactics, and they will feel a great belief in their ability to conquer the obstacle since they have already mastered it.

When a child starts school, they can adapt these problem-solving skills to new social contexts and academic learning. A child with problem-solving solid abilities can take the initiative and weigh actions and consequences to make decisions throughout the school day. They will not be intimidated by new labor or chores but will have the confidence and "can-do" mentality to take on new challenges.

The significance of mastering specific abilities

One of the essential aspects of issue-solving is recognizing a problem at its earliest stage to avoid it from becoming more serious. If a youngster disagrees with a playmate, they must learn the value of sharing and taking turns. This type of knowledge is required for youngsters to form good interpersonal interactions.

Additionally, problem-solving is essential for children's cognitive development. It promotes creativity by allowing children to consider issues from various angles. Sometimes more imaginative answers are preferable to more obvious ones when solving difficulties.

The issues are diverse.

While problem-solving is vital for children's growth, it is essential to remember that not all problems demand the same type of answer (Morin, 2022). Children, for example, would not approach a broken toy as they would an academic task. As a result, it is helpful to remember that there are various types of difficulties, each with its role or purpose.

Physical as well as social problems are the two types of issues that children commonly confront.

Situations like getting food while we are hungry are examples of physical challenges. On the other hand, social issues may include disagreements with friends or siblings and how to react if one of your parents is upset. Understanding the many sorts of disputes will assist youngsters in determining which problem-solving method will work best in each situation.

While learning to solve difficulties is essential to a child's growth, it is not always simple, especially in instances with multiple hurdles. Therefore, a slower approach is typically preferable under challenging situations. This will allow the child to consider many possibilities and assess the benefits and drawbacks.

Kids that easily resolve problems or conflicts have a lot of positive relationships in the future. Furthermore, problem-solving fosters creativity, an essential component of becoming a thriving adult. Children will be better able to develop solutions if they know the various types of difficulties (Morin, 2022).

There are numerous reasons why children's problem-solving abilities are critical. When children can approach and resolve disputes effectively, they use their imaginations, originality, critical thinking, and reasoning to solve a problem. In addition, children who have the opportunity to exercise their problem-solving skills will gain confidence in their talents over time.

When faced with new challenges, youngsters can use reasoning to come up with solutions rather than depending on others for assistance. Self-assurance is the aftermath here. Those that do not face difficulties in relationships. Academically motivated children are less likely to succeed, whereas good problem-solving skills inspire them to participate more actively in the learning process.

3 GENERAL PROBLEM-SOLVING STRATEGIES

Demonstrate effective problem-solving techniques.

When facing a problem, conduct a "think-aloud" for your kid's benefit. Demonstrate how to use the problem-solving techniques you have been practicing together, using real-life examples she may apply in her own life.

Simultaneously, demonstrate to your child a readiness to make mistakes. It is natural for people to have troubles, and that is fine. Likewise, it is perfectly fine if the first solution you try does not work.

Explain that some factors are beyond our control when you are modeling problem-solving. Therefore, when trying to solve a problem, we should concentrate on the aspects we D.O. have control over.

Seek advice.

When you have an issue, seek counsel from your children. This educates kids that making mistakes and facing problems is normal. Furthermore, if you show them that their contributions are good, kids will feel more confident in attempting to solve problems on their own.

Do not Give "The Solution."

Allow your child to fight, sometimes lose, and ultimately benefit from consequences, as painful as they may be. Let us look at some age-appropriate tactics and activities now. The ages stated below are suggestions; feel free to use whatever tactics or actions you think would work best for your child.

13 AGE-APPROPRIATE ACTIVITIES FOR PRACTICING PROBLEM-SOLVING

▷ **3 to 5 years**

Employ Emotional Coaching

Young children must first try to handle their emotions before they can enter a problem-solving attitude. After all, when a tiny child is having a tantrum, it is difficult for him to think correctly about solutions to a problem.

The emotion coaching approach suggested by John Gottman is one way to do this. Teach your children that ALL feelings are normal (Ever, 2022). There are no such things as "bad" feelings. Anger, grief, and frustration, all of which appear to be bad emotions, can teach us valuable things. How we deal is what matters.

Second, follow the steps below:

- Step 1: Name and validate your feelings. When your child is distressed, assist her in processing her feelings. "I understand you are unhappy because Jessica is enjoying the toy you wanted," you could say.
- Step 2: Dealing with your feelings. Assist your youngster in finding her safe haven. Allow her to process her emotions and soothe her body so she can problem-solve, educate, and grow.
- Step 3: Listen more than talk as you brainstorm solutions with your youngster during the dialogue. This enables your child to exercise her problem-solving abilities, and she will be likelier to implement her answers.

"Show Me the Difficult Part," you might say.

Try an approach by mom and parenting writer Lauren Tamm when your child is struggling or frustrated. "Show me the difficult portion," you can simply say. This assists your youngster in identifying the root of the problem, making it less daunting and easier to address.

- "So you are saying..." repeat after your child.

Encourage your child to come up with ideas once you have both grasped the underlying issue. "You can do it!" "I know you can solve it!"

Your youngster will most likely be able to find a solution now that she has identified "the difficult portion." If not, assist her in developing some ideas (Ever, 2022). For example, you may ask her, "If you know, what would you think?" and see what she says.

Problem-solving through imaginative play

Allow your child to select activities and games that she enjoys. Free play provides numerous options to navigate and solve challenges creatively (Ever, 2022). Kids learn from playing, and this is not something new. Playing with blocks, basic puzzles, and dress-up clothes can help your youngster learn how to solve problems.

Even when playing, your youngster considers the following questions: Where does this puzzle piece go? What is the purpose of this? I would like to dress up like a queen for Halloween. So, what should I put on? What happened to my tiara? Is it hidden beneath the couch?

Storybooks can help you solve problems.

Reading age-appropriate tales about characters who are dealing with issues, such as:

- Jacky Davis's *Ladybug Girl & Bumblebee Boy* tells the story of two pals who want to play together but cannot decide on a game. They come up with a game they both wish to play after taking turns providing suggestions.
- Margaret and H.E. Rey's *Curious George* Series: A curious little monkey gets into and out of sticky situations, teaching children how to solve their difficulties.
- Bernard Waber's *Ira Sleeps Over*: The one called Ira is afraid and does not want to spend the night at his best friend's house. However, there is one problem: should he bring his teddy bear or not? It may seem insignificant, but this is the early social issue your child may be exposed to.

Connect these events to similar occurrences in your child's life, and ask questions to your child regarding the characters that solved their difficulties. Then, encourage various alternatives and discuss how they might turn out (Ever, 2022).

This is a type of dialogue reading in which you actively engage your child in the reading process. In preschool-aged kids, engaging with the text rather than simply listening might "turbocharge" the growth of literacy skills such as comprehension.

You can help your child's problem-solving skills by asking questions regarding the characters' issues. Then, to emphasize the lesson, have your youngster role-play the problem and possible remedies to emphasize the lesson.

▷ 5 to 7 years

Teach the Steps to Solve a Problem

Create a simple problem-solving approach for your child that you can use regularly. For instance, consider the following five steps:

- Step 1: How am I feeling right now? Assist your youngster in comprehending her current emotions (frustration, curiosity, anger, excitement, disappointment, happiness). Noticing and labeling emotions will help your child de-escalate their feelings and take a step back.
- Step 2: What exactly is the issue? Assist your youngster in identifying the exact problem. Instead of pointing fingers, try to assist her in accepting responsibility for what happened. For example, instead of saying, "Joey got me in trouble at recess," your youngster could say, "I got in trouble for disagreeing with Joey at recess."
- Step 3: What are the options for resolving the problem? Urge your child to think of as many ideas as possible (Ever, 2022). They should not even be amazing. They are only having a brainstorming session right now and are not yet assessing the ideas they have come up with.

- Step 4: Scenarios. What would happen if your youngster tried all of these ideas? Is the solution secure and equitable? What effect will it have on others? Role-playing is fine here as well. However, your child must consider both her behavior's positive and negative implications.
- Step 5: Which will I try first? Request that your youngster chooses one or more options to test. If the remedy did not work, figure out why and try again. Encourage your youngster to persevere in their efforts until the problem is solved.

Practice these procedures repeatedly until they become part of the routine, then model how to solve problems similarly. What worked and what did not work? Think about where things went wrong and what you would do differently in the future.

Using Craft Materials to Solve a Problem

Another type of play that can educate kids to handle difficulties imaginatively is crafting. Brushes, modeling clay, storage boxes, tape, paper, and other materials should be available to your child. With these basic resources, they will develop various unique inventions and activities. Some "open-ended toys" do not have a "correct" way to play, allowing your youngster to be creative and develop their ideas.

Pose open-ended questions to your audience.

Asking open-ended questions helps children think critically and imaginatively, which allows them to solve problems more effectively. Here are some examples:

- How could we collaborate to find a solution?
- What method did you use to figure it out? How did you figure that out?
- Tell me about the things you have built, made, or made.
- What do you anticipate will happen next, in your opinion?
- What do you believe will happen if...?
- What did you discover?
- What was the easiest part? What was the most challenging part?
- What differently would you do if you could do it all over again?

There is no right or wrong answer to an open-ended question, and it cannot be replied with a simple "Yes" or "No." Even if your child is not presently solving an issue, you can offer open-ended questions to help them practice their thinking abilities, which will be helpful when she has a challenge.

▷ **7-10 years**

Decompose Problems into Chunks

Your child's issues grow in proportion to her size. Encourage your youngster to break down a challenge that looks overwhelming or impossible into smaller, more manageable parts. For example, let us imagine your youngster had a low grade in history class. Why did this lousy grade happen? What is the reason? What are the underlying causes of this issue?

Listen to your child's brainstorming session; if she gets stuck, offer open-ended questions. If your kid's low grade is due to missed assignments, have him, or her make a note of them and work on them one at a time. What is causing your kid to suffer on exams if tests are the issue?

Perhaps she is preoccupied with classmates, has difficulty looking for assistance, and does not devote enough time to studying at home. Once you have recognized these "chunks," assist your youngster in tackling them one by one until the issue is resolved.

Include the "The Broken Escalator Video"

The "broken escalator video" talks about the necessity of accepting challenges and addressing difficulties on your own. An escalator abruptly breaks in the video. The escalator passengers are "stuck" and yelling for assistance. At this age, your youngster is likely to find the movie amusing and provide an instant answer: "Just walk!" "Off the escalator!" says the narrator.

Explain to your child that this is only one example of how individuals behave in challenging situations. "Why do you believe they did not get off the escalator?" you might inquire. (they did not realize how they require help, etcetera.)

When your child confronts issues, they may feel "stuck." As a result, they may come to a halt and seek assistance before attempting to solve the problem. Instead, inspire your child to take on challenges and solve difficulties.

Solve a Problem Using Prompts

Provide straws, cotton balls, thread, clothespins, glue, paper clips, notepads, sticky notes, popsicle sticks, and other supplies to your child or a group of children. Challenge your children to solve unique challenges using only these materials, such as:

- Construct a leprechaun trap.
- Construct an automobile jump ramp.
- Create your own set of rules for a game.
- Construct a device that allows two people to communicate with each other.

Problem-solving is another fantastic method of critical thinking. It will almost certainly take several efforts to find a viable solution that can apply to nearly every element of life.

Make them earn it by making them work for it.

When your child requests a new toy, piece of technology, or outfit, have her build a plan to get it on her own. Your child will not only have to think and assess solutions, but she will also build confidence. Also, encourage your child as it works toward their goal by asking her how they can earn money for the item they desire.

Put your ideas on paper.

Make your child write down their difficulties and brainstorm some possible answers on paper. However, she now takes things a step further: Which solutions worked after you tried them all? Which ones did not work out? Why? This allows your youngster to consider different outcomes and learn what works and does not. She can apply what she has learned here when she runs into similar issues in the future.

Pictionary as a group

Teamwork is an essential ability for people of all ages. It is a talent that children and young adults employ, not only during the school day but also outside of school, such as during a sporting event or when playing a game alongside friends at home. In addition, kids learn other vital skills such as communication, listening, turn-taking, performing a fair portion of the work, and disagreeing completely while learning to work as a team. These are not just classroom talents; they are life skills as well.

Allow each team to choose an artist to sketch for them. Next, allow the artists to select a card with a phrase they must illustrate on paper or the board. Allow both artists to draw at the exact moment as their teammates try to determine which sentence they are painting. The hitch is that the artist can only create visuals, not words, so the team must collaborate to figure out what the artist is painting. The team that correctly guesses the sentence first is the winner! The game can be repeated as needed, with different group members are chosen each time.

Board Game for Social Communication

Small talk with a student in the corridor, reading nonverbal clues, having a lengthy conversation with friends at lunch, and using our social filter before speaking are all examples. Our ability to communicate significantly impacts how we interact with others and form connections over time.

This game is excellent for youngsters, especially those struggling with social language. Children will have to read social signs from a real-life photo, debate what they would do or say in a situation, and indicate how they ought to think before speaking or reciting a specific sentence in a range of tones, depending on which space they fall into. Because there are over 150 different cards, kids may play over and over while honing their skills.

That is when the chapter comes to a close. Children can benefit from problem-solving skills in a variety of situations. They will also be able to persevere in the face of adversity.

In a child's development, problem-solving is critical. This crucial ability entails more than just coming up with a solution. Instead, it involves employing one's imagination, pondering possibilities, reasoning through plans or pathways, and applying logic to complex problems or queries.

Confronting confidence issues can also help children feel more excellent about themselves and have improved self-esteem. It is also necessary for future academic achievement. Forming relationships with others may be difficult if a child lacks social skills.

Learning to tackle problems takes practice, which can help you stay motivated and improve your grades! Finally, we have arrived at the book's final chapter, which discusses the significance of good manners.

9

USING MANNERS

 It is difficult, but educating your children's manners is vital. It is essential beyond please and thank you. Getting youngsters into the habit of employing politeness at a young age, like so many other things, makes life much easier in the long run (Eilidh, 2022).

As my children grow older and begin to play outside the home and engage with teachers and parents, I have noticed that they do not always make eye contact and frequently forget to say, "excuse me." I have also discovered that encouraging children to use excellent manners is insufficient.

To instill good manners in children, they must understand why they are vital. They see their parents and how they act.

This is how they know what people do, what is right, and what is wrong.

Their eyes brighten up with understanding as I explain why specific manners exist. They say, "Ohhhh." "All right!" They begin to put it into practice. Start implementing the manners you want to see in your children first.

They are paying much attention, even if it is something you do not want them to. Here are the 11 most essential manners for kids and my explanations for why they are vital.

While many may appear basic sense, children do not understand what is expected of them unless you explain it. So clear your expectations, and then lead by example so that students can see decent manners in action.

THE 11 MUST-KNOW MANNERS

- Saying "please." This demonstrates that you care about other people.
- Express gratitude. This conveys thankfulness and appreciation.
- When speaking to others, look them in the eyes. It is a friendly method to communicate that you care about the other person.
- Express regret. It demonstrates empathy and a willingness to accept responsibility for your actions.

- Smile and maintain a positive attitude. This is beneficial to both yourself and others!
- Engage in light conversation. This is a crucial social skill for forming and maintaining friendships and finding and retaining a job later in life.
- Ask other questions. In this way, you express interest.
- Sincerely apologize. This demonstrates that you care about other people.
- Keep your eyes peeled for opportunities to appreciate others. This improves reciprocal relationships by making others feel good.
- Sharing. This demonstrates your concern for others and encourages you to consider others, allowing you to appreciate what you have.
- Always treat other people in the way you want to be treated.

Your kid will notice when you speak respectfully to others and use your manners. That is why you need to be a positive model. Pay close attention to how you talk with other people around you, especially your partner. It is easy to overlook using proper etiquette when you are around people you know well.

Show different ways of kindness with cards, ask for stuff in the most respectful way possible, and do not forget always to show gratitude. Do not forget that your kids are constantly watching you. No matter the location or the company.

Situations in which you are upset are the most crucial ones. If you like to yell when you are upset, stop doing that, or at least stop doing it in front of your child. Likewise, your message on the importance of having or improving good manners will be lost if you do not show polite and respectful behavior.

A simple explanation is enough.

Do not preach, do not include long stories! Instead, politely explain why the behavior will not be tolerated or praised (Eilidh, 2022). Tell your child that people do not like speaking to others while eating or having full mouths.

Without intention, you may be the one that encourages the activity. So do not make a big deal out of it! Remember, you change the whole scenario and your child's perspective by saying things differently or more calmly.

When you give a quick explanation of why a particular behavior is considered unfriendly or unpleasant, kids are more likely to recall their manners, including specific etiquette standards.

Have Age-Appropriate Standards

"Please"

"Thank you"

"Sorry"

- These are the first manners your toddler should learn. A fantastic place to start.

Before moving on to the part with the exercises and activities, it is sometimes good to concentrate on one area at a time, such as basic table manners. Go slowly because learning all at once scares children. It is also a good idea to go over previous skills with your child now and again to make sure they remember how to use them.

As part of your daily family life, you can assist your child in learning how to be a good friend.

For instance, when playing with a sibling, your child may need to bargain over what to play with or who receives which object. You can discuss and explain what is going on and why when these circumstances occur. "That was a terrific idea to listen to each other before deciding what to do," for example, or "How about telling a narrative where you both took a turn with the toy?"

Friendship requires talking and listening abilities, such as expressing interest in what others are saying and asking questions. Family dinners are an excellent opportunity to display these skills and allow your child to practice them.

Another skill you may demonstrate and your child can practice during family activities is how to win and lose graciously. This is when family board games come in handy. Do not forget that these abilities are complex sometimes, even for you. Your kid is still learning and requires much practice in being a good buddy.

18 FUN ACTIVITIES AND GAMES FOR MANNERS

Play role-playing games with the following scenarios:

At a table, two kids are coloring. One of the children requires a crayon that is out of reach. However, it is within the other child's grasp. What should the first youngster tell the second child closest to the crayons? (Assign two children to act out this scene.)

The kids are waiting in line at the water fountain. Another child approaches the second child and asks for "cuts" in line. The teacher is providing instructions, and one of the students in the class has a query concerning the instructions. Together, determine the best action when some of these things happen.

It is a chilly day outdoors, and one of the children is dressed in a sweater and a coat. The second child wears just a shirt and shorts. What should the child with the warmer clothes do? Set an example.

Thank you, and please.

There are many people in the world, and excellent manners make it easier for everyone to get along. So make sure you teach this or place it on a paper that they can see and read:

- We say "please" when we ask for anything and "thank you" when someone offers us something.
- We all know that when it is time for lunch, we wash our arms and sit upright at the table.
- We also understand that speaking with our mouths full is impolite.
- When we exercise together, everyone enjoys themselves because we share and are courteous to one another.
- It is not acceptable to whisper about those close by while playing with our pals since it may harm their feelings.
- Interrupting someone who is trying to speak is impolite.
- Everyone admires someone with decent manners. Good manners make everyone happy and make you a pleasant person to be around.

Time for questions

- What do you say if you accidentally walk in front of someone? "Excuse me."
- How can you name the activity that includes you moving up a little so another kid can sit down? "Sharing"
- "Please" is what you say when you ask for something.
- You say "thank you" when you get something from someone.

Write those "laws" on pasteboard throughout your house or classroom, and each day we give an area to someone who helps everyone else recall how to use their manners.

Game of Manners

You will need a collection of photographs (cut from magazines) depicting toddlers or adults expressing each emotion. Glue to heavy construction paper or cardstock pieces that are the same size. Number Some children cannot express themselves verbally. If infants are to comprehend their emotional states, kids must hear words like "happy," "sad," "mad," and "nervous."

Hold up one of the photographs during cycle time and ask the kids how this individual is feeling. (Tell them if they do not know.) Invite the kids to talk about what they observe that inspires them—stack at least three photographs of each emotion on an activity table (Burnett, 2021). Rearrange the photos in a different sequence. One kid should be given the stack and should collect together all of the pictures. Show numerous photographs depicting the same feeling at a table or during circle time and ask the students to determine how each person feels.

Puppets Who Are Polite

Small paper boxes, marking markers, rubber glue, scissors, and construction paper are all items you will need (Burnett, 2021). Puppets appeal to children because they allow them to imagine being someone else without fear of judgment.

You should make a sample puppet using a little paper bag whose face represents one of the fundamental emotions. Place supplies on a table in the art area and encourage the kids to make their own joyful, sad, angry, or confused faces. Interested in doing more: Make a puppet family with each puppet expressing a distinct emotion. Use these dolls to perform short skits for the audience.

Miss Bee doll

Maintain this activity in mind if you want your kids to start making decisions about proper behavior. Make a Miss Bee doll (Burnett, 2021) for each youngster first. Draw a grinning face on one yellow paper platter and a gloomy face on the other plate to form one. Two craft sticks should be black. To mimic antennas, cut two small circles from black colored paper and glue one to one end of each.

Connect the backs of both plates with glue. Allow each child to utilize his puppet during this team time activity when he has completed his puppet. Describe a circumstance in which right or bad manners were applied using the following suggestions. Let each child make its doll according to the situation you are in - a sad one or a happy one. Encourage volunteers to create their scenarios after applying the suggestions below. Make sure to include the following:

- When Glass Grasshopper received a treat, she said, "Thank you."
- Bobby Bumblebee accidentally knocked his brother out of the hive.
- Pippie the Ant stood in line and waited her turn.
- Petar Caterpillar silently ate.
- Melly, the Caterpillar, spoke with a full mouth. Is this right? How would you correct it?
- Solka Spider was a spider who liked to play with his meals. Is this right? How would you correct it?
- Chanser Cricket chirped in the background while another cricket chirped. Before interrupting, Casy Cricket tweeted, "Excuse me."
- Lucy Ladybug took a leaf without asking permission. Is this right? How would you correct it?

A Game of Honey

This delightful game can help your little one practice saying "please" and "thank you." Cut a honeycomb shape out of yellow construction paper ahead of time, then add features using a marker (Burnett, 2021). Take out the straw hat and sit it in a chair. Make sure it does not face the children involved.

Solicit a volunteer to sit in the chair, put on the hat, and act as Miss Bee. Underneath the chair, place the honeycomb. Then, Miss Bee should close her eyes. After that, select another child to come to the chair. Let the child join others.

As Miss Bee turns to face the gathering, she opens her eyes. Recite the following chant:

> (Kids) Miss Bee Polite, you are a lovely young lady.
> Could we have a honey treat, please?
> "Yes, you may," Miss Bee Polite Doll responded.
> (Kids) We all say, "Thank you, thank you."

If necessary, give Miss Bee multiple chances to figure out who took the honeycomb before revealing the youngster. Miss Bee is the child who snatched the honeycomb. Repeat until each youngster is crowned queen bee.

Housekeeping Etiquette

Place a jar of cereal, napkins, little paper napkins, and a spoon in the hour housekeeping area. Miss Bee should be placed in the center of the table. Encourage each youngster to sit at the table, grab a napkin and a plate, and scoop a mouthful of cereal for himself. Remind children that Miss Bee will be on the lookout for good table manners.

Pledge of Kindness

Constantly ask your children what it means to be kind, a friend, or friendly, whatever term they like. Write them down, and then make a song out of them. Make sure it is simple and uses words they will understand. After all, that is the point of fully comprehending the game's backstory.

Obstacle Course Collaboration

Make an obstacle course for the kids and have them go through it in one way. Remind the kids about taking turns nicely — this is great practice for kids with problems waiting for slower kids ahead of them.

Friendship Is a Gift

Remind the kids how nice it feels to offer someone a present and have them respond with gratitude. What are some methods to express your appreciation? "Thank you," "it is lovely!" "It is just what I was looking for," "I adore it!" Draw names and have the kids prepare a present (image) for the person whose name they drew. Give the gift to their friend. Then, using markers or crayons for the artwork, have the kids construct thank you cards.

Chart of Etiquette

You should also develop a chart with your children and encourage the children to help you think of occasions where saying "please" and "thank you" is necessary (Burnett, 2021) (for example, please pass the salt), which we then place on the board.

Keep your hands to yourself if you want to be successful

I told my kids that we should keep our hands to ourselves (no shoving, no invading other people's space). The kids then use a piece of colored paper to paint their handprints.

Sharing

Each child should bring a toy or other unique item to "share" with the rest of the class or their brothers and sisters. Often speak about how sharing things makes us feel good.

Shared Colors

Make a cup of colored water for each child–red for one, blue for another, and yellow for the third. Take empty cups, add water to each and start to tell them that by mixing it up (sharing colors), they could make another different, better color.

Let's Take a Look

Take the kids for a walk, and when they come home, talk about the new sounds you observed, what you spoke about on the walk, and so on. Let it be a simple, open conversation.

Cover up and keep the yuck at bay

"Cover your nose when you sneeze" is a fantastic thing to start with. Read it first. Second, give the children a paper plate and tell them to draw a self-portrait (Burnett, 2021). Since I already did this, I traced their hands on colored paper, put a kleenex on top, and glued the hand cutout onto the paper plate (over the nose of their painting).

Fun with the Sharing Box

Create a sharing box for each youngster with two or three toys. Put the toy on the floor. Let the children pick a toy. Set a timer in the kitchen to go off after a specific time. When the timer goes off, have the kids put their toys back in the box and choose new ones (Burnett, 2021). Then ring the timer bell once more.

10

MAKING AND KEEPING FRIENDS

 Most children's routines include having a best friend, interacting with other children, and attending birthday parties. According to the American Academy of Pediatrics, "making new friends is one of the most crucial goals of childhood development and social skills that will last a lifetime." Friendships help children develop emotionally as well as morally, as well as improve their social abilities.

Children learn not only how to interact with others (Sollo-van, 2022), but solid friendships can also help them try to handle their emotions and share their feelings appropriately. Some kids, however, suffer socially and have difficulty developing and maintaining friends.

HOW TO ASSIST CHILDREN IN MAKING FRIENDS

Although friendship is a crucial component of life, not every child is born with the ability to make new friends, which is perfectly fine. However, it can be upsetting for both of you if your child does not appear to have friends or is occasionally (or never) asked to play with other children. There are numerous ways you may assist children (Sollovan, 2022) in navigating their social environment and developing meaningful friendships.

WHY ARE FRIENDSHIPS IMPORTANT?

Making friends is crucial to growing older and a child's emotional and social development. Thanks to friends, children can develop high levels of confidence and self-esteem. Positive connections may also act as a barrier against bullying.

According to some studies, getting quality friends may help prevent bullies and, in circumstances where bullying occurs, may make it much easier for youngsters to deal with. Friendships, especially healthy ones, teach us a lot.

This creates a sense of identity and belonging. Peer pressure becomes good in these settings, especially when children push one another to develop an interest in charity and social justice.

Furthermore, friendships are essential at practically every age. Even toddlers appear to play together and make friends, even though group play does not completely develop until the age of three.

As a result, it is never too early to assist your youngster in developing friendship skills. If you are unsure whether your child has friends, speak with their instructors about how they interact with other students at school. You can also inquire about your child's friendships to better understand how well they are establishing friends.

Also, if they are content with the number of friends they have, they should avoid making the concept of acquiring friends a more significant concern than it needs to be. Once you have determined how your child feels—whether they are happy or unhappy—you can devise a strategy to help them improve the social skills required to form healthy connections. The abilities you can hone with them

Improve your child's Conversation Skills

Learning how to start and maintain discussions with others is a talent your child may need to perfect, from taking turns while chatting to posing questions about others. Until your youngster learns to pick up on signs from people during a conversation intuitively, arm them with inquiries like "Do you have a hobby?" or "Do you have a pet?" You can also utilize television shows to demonstrate how individuals have polite interactions. Body language, voice tone, and interruptions in the dialogue are all crucial cues when communicating with others. Role-playing interactions can help kids gain the necessary practice.

Work on your child's listening skills.

Being a good friend entails having strong social skills and understanding how to show an interest in another individual. As a result, you should build on your child's willingness to hear and sympathize with others. Discuss with your youngster how to recognize when somebody is going through a difficult period.

Teach them how to extend other kindness. For example, your child could bake cookies for a friend's sick pet or write a note to someone who has lost a loved one. Taking the time to show someone you care is an excellent method to demonstrate empathy to a possible new acquaintance.

Look for Chances to Meet Peers

If your child lacks friends, they might not have enough opportunities to make them. Participating in various activities with kids their age who share similar interests might be a terrific way to make new friends. In addition, it may be beneficial to provide your child with additional chances to meet kids with whom they will bond.

Let your child be a part of groups and other non-school activities. Be aware of your child's level of energy as well as their traits. Let them recharge. You should also urge your children to make friends with others who are different from them.

- If your kid is having difficulty deciding what they like and dislike, you might make a recommendation to see if anything sounds appetizing. You could try:
- Tennis, tai chi, swimming, or a jogging club are examples of individual sports.
- Music and art courses, robotics classes, or clubs are non-competitive activities.
- Book clubs or story-times at your local library, bookshop, parks, pools, playgrounds, trampoline parks, and other general play areas.
- Volunteer activities such as a local food bank or a community clean-up program where they can work alongside other children are available.
- Team sports such as football, soccer, tennis, and volleyball are examples of youth sports and classes.

If you are worried your child is nervous about meeting new people, do not give up. Let your child bring an icebreaker, like a pet, snacks, or toys for assistance. This is particularly beneficial if your child is not typically outgoing.

3 FUN ACTIVITIES THAT COULD ASSIST IN MAKING FRIENDS

Friendship at a Glance (Sollovan, 2022)

This brief encounter allows children to discover more about their classmates and make friends immediately.

Chairs, a whiteboard, and erasable markers are required.

With chairs, form two circles: an inner circle looking out and an outermost ring facing in. In pairs, the chairs should meet each other. Allow each child to select a chair. When it is time to "go," the kids have three minutes to ask one another the following questions (write them down first):

- What is your favorite class?
- What is the worst thing that you did?
- What is your favorite sport?
- Where would you prefer to live - a city or a village? Why?

Make the inner circle move circular, and the outer circle rotates counterclockwise every three minutes. Kids start over and ask the same question in this game.

Connecting the Dots (Sollovan, 2022)

This hilarious game will encourage kids to collaborate and make friends. Gather the children in the center of the room. Tell them you will provide instructions on connecting with others in a group. Children who do not associate with a group are seated until the next round. Say how much children should play and what they should do. For example, a group of six kids should be touching elbows. As the kids work together and form relationships, this game will generate a lot of laughter and pleasure.

Special Stores (Sollovan, 2022)

With this practice, children enjoy showcasing their hobbies and talents. The kids will need pencils, paper, and shop supplies for this.

Instruct children to jot down their top three hobbies or interests. Then, pair children together based on their interests and have them collaborate to establish a "store" during classes for a few weeks. For example, kids who prefer doing hair and nails could own a beauty salon, or if they adore a specific sport, they could open a pro shop. Give the kids materials and time to set up their stores. After the stores are completed, pretend money and divide each group into two mini-groups: shoppers and servers. Allow each group of shoppers to go shopping for one week while the servers assist them at their stores. The following week, switch shoppers and servers. Your children will make friends through working with individuals who share their interests.

FINAL WORDS

This book emphasized that learning these nine essential skills will allow your child to grow into a much calmer and more loving adult. Each skill teaches your child a different discipline through interactions, exercises, and games appropriate for their age.

This method is not only better for your children, their future, and your relationship with them, but it also improves their social skills and makes your life easier by increasing the collaboration you will receive from your children.

Even with the finest intentions and the most deliberate approaches, everyone might come away from a disciplinary encounter furious, confused, and dissatisfied. Therefore, we aim to give messages of hope and peace in our closing pages for those terrible moments we all inevitably confront as we discipline our children and teach them the life skills they need.

Do not be afraid, do not hesitate to implement the changes, and trust me, everything will be okay. However, the challenging moments should teach you that your child is alive and that they could do better and learn how.

Moments like these underscore a truth that all parents should be aware of - there are times when there is nothing we can do about many things when our children are having difficulties. We can make an effort to be calm and loving. We can be fully present and have complete access to our creative potential. Even so, we may not be able to improve matters immediately. When our children go through difficult emotions, all we can do is be present. When children desire to be alone, we can respect what they believe they need to relax.

This is not to say that we would leave a weeping child alone in his room for an extended period. And it does not mean we do not attempt new approaches when our youngster requires assistance. We can always get in touch.

Our children will ultimately soften and quiet down, even without a magic wand. They will eventually be able to detect our good intentions and accept our affection and comfort. We reconnect when they do. And, even though we will continue to make mistakes as parents because we are human, we can always go to our children and mend the gap.

LEAVE A ONE-CLICK REVIEW

I hope that you have enjoyed this book.
If you like this book, please leave a review on Amazon.
It will take a few seconds to do.
Just scan the QR code or visit the link below !

http://www.Amazon.com/review/create-review?&asin=
B0B7KCFKGR

By doing this you will really help get the book out there to
potential readers that would massively benefit from it.

Thank you very much.

- Kate Herm

REFERENCES

Amy Morin, L. C. S. W. (2021, April 13). *How to Teach Kids Problem-Solving Skills* Verywell Family. Retrieved June 14, 2022, from https://www.very wellfamily.com/teach-kids-problem-solving-skills-1095015

Coulson, J. (2017). *7 Ways to Teach Your Child Self-Control*. Happy Families. Retrieved June 14, 2022, from https://www.happyfamilies.com.au/arti cles/7-ways-to-teach-your-child-self-control

Korte, B. (2016*). Body Language In Literature*. In Body Language in Literature. University of Toronto Press.

Eilidh, J. (n.d.). *Importance of problem-solving in Child Development*. Mrs. Myers Reading Room. Retrieved June 14, 2022, from https://mrsmyersrr.com/ news/importance-problem-solving-child-development

Ever, T. (2022, January 19). *5-Step Problem Solving for Young Children*. Heart. Retrieved June 14, 2022, from https://heartmindonline.org/resources/5-step-problem-solving-for-young-children

Jodi Burnett. (2021, August 19). *8 Problem Solving Games to Play With Your Preschooler*. Atlas Mission. Retrieved June 14, 2022, from https://www. atlasmission.com/blog/8-problem-solving-games-play-preschooler/

O'NEILL, K. A. (2002). *Kids speak effective communication with the school-aged/adolescent patient*. Pediatric emergency care, 18(2), 137-140.

Trewa, F. (n.d.). *10 Fun Activities Teaching Empathy at Home and School*. Fun and Function. Retrieved June 14, 2020, from https://funandfunction.com/ blog/need-empathy-10-fun-activities-for-home-or-school

Sears, D. B. S. D., & Sears, D. B. (2020, September 21). *11 Ways to Teach Your Child to Share*. Ask Dr. Sears. Retrieved June 14, 2022, from https://www. askdrsears.com/topics/parenting/discipline-behavior/morals-manners/ 11-ways-teach-your-child-share/

Sollovan, B. (n.d.). *Have We Lost Our Manners? 5 Important Social Skills All Kids Need to Master*. ParentMap. Retrieved June 14, 2022, from https://www. parentmap.com/article/5-important-social-skills-all-kids-need-master

Weng, M. (2015, November 3). *The 10 Top Friendship Games and Activities*.

Healthline. Retrieved June 14, 2022, from https://www.healthline.com/
health/parenting/friendship-activities#Preschool-Friendship-Activities

Made in United States
North Haven, CT
02 August 2023

39834389R00093